WONDERS OF MAN

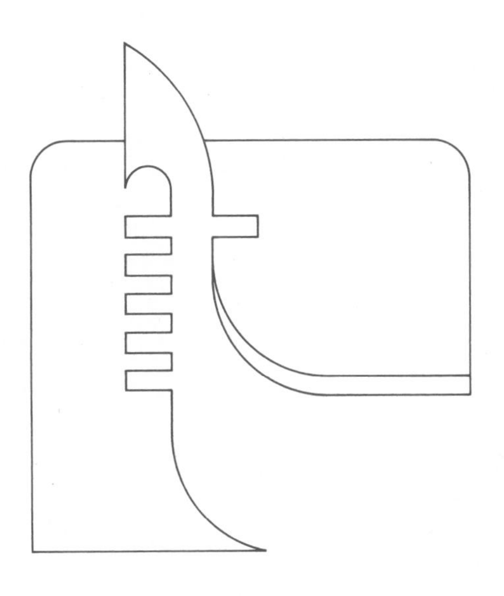

PAX
TIBI
MAR

VENICE

by John H. Davis
and the Editors
of the Newsweek Book Division

NEWSWEEK, New York

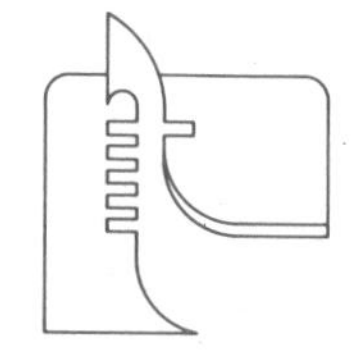

Opposite:
Close-up of the renowned bronze horses — Roman in origin and timeless in style — that grace the parapet of the basilica

Endpapers:
A geometrically patterned detail from the inlaid stone floor of St. Mark's Basilica

Title Page:
The scarlet and gold flag of the city of Venice unfurled above the domes of St. Mark's

ISBN: Clothbound Edition 0–88225–028–0
ISBN: Deluxe Edition 0–88225–029–9
Library of Congress Catalog Card No. 72–75997

Contents

Introduction

Rarely in human history has a vigorous and progressive civilization arisen in a less likely place than the mud flats of the Venetian lagoon. Curiously enough, it was the very inaccessibility of the area that attracted men to it in the sixth century A.D., for it provided the city's founders with a reedy, water-girded refuge from the barbarians who had invaded their mainland homes. For those invaders from central Asia, who were unable to swim and reluctant to sail, the shallow lagoon had proved an uncrossable gulf — and as a result, the islands of the Rivo Alto, upon which Venice stands, became a haven for thousands of aristocratic refugees from the Italian mainland.

Reacting to adversity with industry and ingenuity, those displaced patricians created a maritime empire of unparalleled splendor. At its zenith, the Republic of Venice was said to encompass "one quarter and one half of one quarter" of the known world. During those years her wealth and beauty literally beggared description, and her merchant princess lived more lavishly than many kings. With the discovery of the New World, however, Venice's trading monopolies were broken. The long, slow decline that followed — aptly labeled Venice's "golden sunset" by the author of the ensuing narrative — was protracted and infinitely poignant. Today, the decaying buildings adjoining the Rialto Bridge (right) serve as haunting reminders of a bygone age when Venice was called La Serenissima, the Most Serene Republic. Industrial pollutants and general neglect now threaten the very fabric of the city that was once known as the most beautiful in the world — the bride of the Adriatic and the unchallenged mistress of the Mediterranean.

THE EDITORS

HOTEL RIALTO
RESTAURANT
143

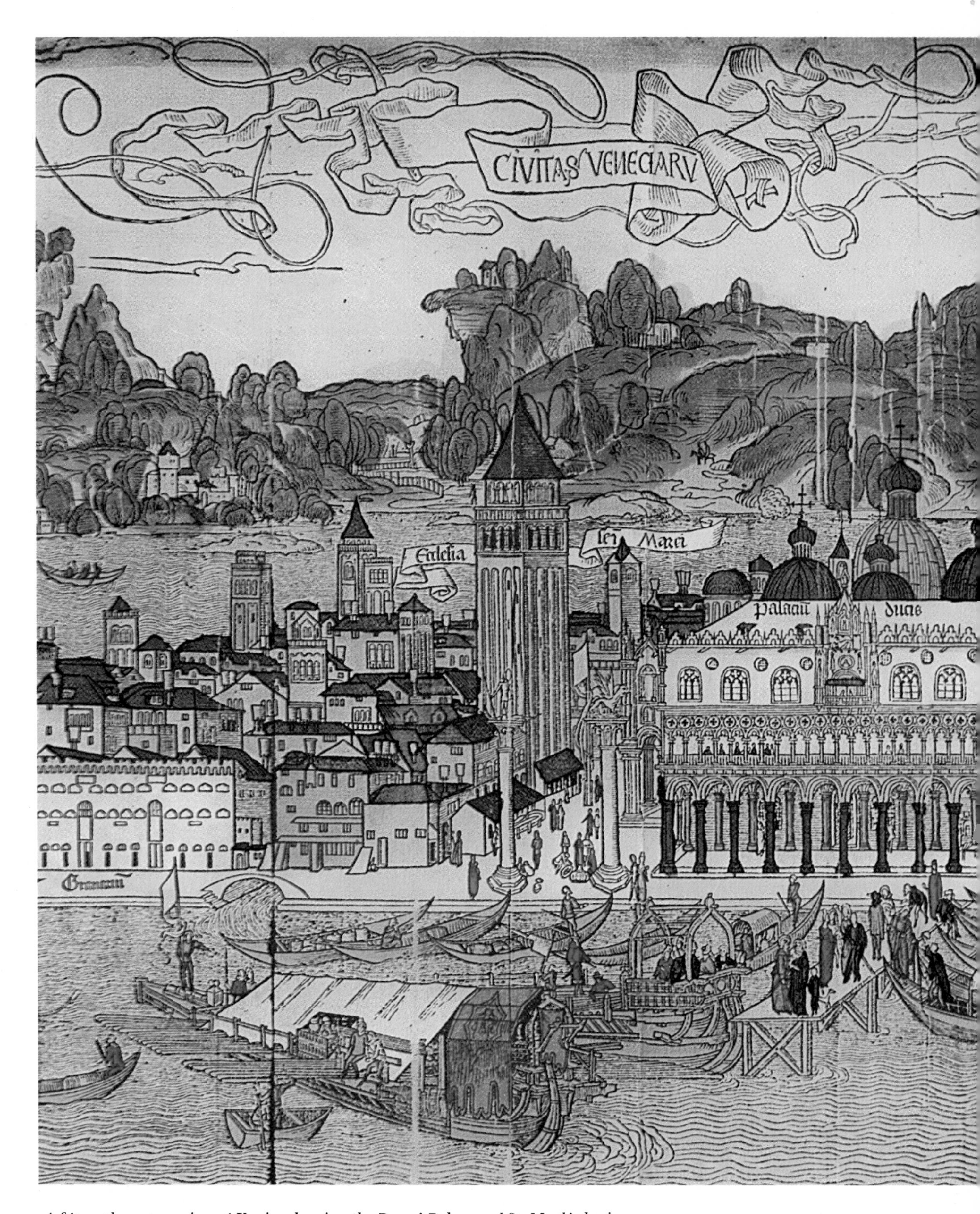

A fifteenth-century view of Venice showing the Doges' Palace and St. Mark's basin

VENICE IN HISTORY

I

The Birth of Venice

The most triumphant city I ever set eyes on" — such was Phillipe de Commynes's impression of Venice in 1495. The widely traveled French nobleman and ambassador was not exaggerating. At the time of his visit, Venice was a world power, the strongest city-state in Italy, one of the richest states in Europe, and the dominant naval power in the Mediterranean. Her mainland frontier extended from Lake Como in the west to Trieste in the east — embracing such cities as Verona, Vicenza, Padua, Bergamo, Brescia, and Treviso — and her overseas empire reached all the way to Turkey. She owned the Dalmatian coast, part of Albania, all of Corfu, most of the Ionian islands, several ports on the Peloponnesus, Crete, Cyprus, several Aegean islands, and a large stretch of Anatolia. In addition, she held entire quarters in such wealthy cities as Alexandria, Jerusalem, Sidon, and Tyre, and she owned trading posts as far away as the Black Sea and the Indian Ocean. Her empire's population of 3,500,000 was larger than that of Great Britain, and her doge, or chief magistrate, was able to boast that he was ruler of "one quarter and a half of one quarter of the Roman Empire."

The island city itself was the greatest marketplace and clearinghouse in the Western world and the principal port of entry in Europe for the commodities of Arabia, China, and the Indies. Virtually anything could be bought or sold in fifteenth-century Venice: spices, gold, oil, slaves, silk, wild animals, jewels, hides, tin, copper, steel, brocades, ivory, ebony, galleons, paintings, mosaics. Entire fleets were moored along the Venetian quays. By the end of the fifteenth century, the value of Venice's exports totaled 12,000,000 ducats a year, of which 5,000,000 were clear profit.

The center of this vast commercial enterprise was the Rialto, the Wall Street of its day and one of the settings in Shakespeare's *The Merchant of Venice.* In porticoes around the Rialto's Piazza San Giacometto, hundreds of goldsmiths, jewel merchants, money changers, and commodity brokers conducted business. They in turn were surrounded by endless shops and *fondaci,* or warehouse-hotels. The huge *fondaco* of the Germans, which was filled with Swabians, Prussians, Saxons, and every conceivable variety of merchandise, stood just beyond the Rialto Bridge. On either side of the bridge, the banks of the Grand Canal were jammed with hundreds of trading vessels, and the quays swarmed with porters. The bustle was incessant, and it often extended well into the night. No port in Europe could compare with Venice in her heyday, not even Genoa or Bruges, her chief trading rivals on the continent.

The other great center of the island city was the immense Piazza San Marco. Here stood the republic's most important church, the Basilica of St. Mark, focus of both religious devotion and patriotic feeling for the Venetians, and the Doges' Palace, seat of the republic's highly efficient, paternalistic government. In the sumptuous state rooms of the Doges' Palace hung scores of paintings depicting heroic episodes of Venetian history. The titles of some of these gigantic canvases give us an idea of what the Venetians thought of themselves: *Venice Triumphant, Venice Ruling the World, The Apotheosis of Venice, Venice, the Queen of the Adriatic,* and canvases depicting Venetian victories over the Franks, the Greeks, the infidels, the Genoese, the Paduans, and the Albanians.

By 1495 the Most Serene Republic, as Venice liked to call herself, ruled not only the world of commerce but also the world of art and architecture, having constructed on her home islands some of the most splendid buildings, bridges, and squares the world had ever seen. Late-fifteenth-century Venice was a seemingly miraculous vision of gleaming domes, stately towers, ornate bridges, graceful piazzas, elaborate marble palaces – "a compressed splendor," wrote the Swiss art historian Jacob Burckhardt, "where the richest decoration did not hinder the practical employment of every corner of space." Working to adorn these structures were some of the greatest painters of all time: Gentile and Giovanni Bellini, Carlo Crivelli, Vittore Carpaccio, Cima da Conegliano, and the incomparable Giorgione – who were soon to be joined by Titian, Veronese, and Tintoretto. It has been said that no people in history, not even the Florentines or the Flemish, ever lavished so much time and money on the embellishment of their city as did the Venetians in the fifteenth and sixteenth centuries. In so doing they made Venice one of the supreme monuments of Western man.

The visual splendor of Venice in 1495 was not confined to painting, sculpture, and architecture alone, however. Venice was also a city of gorgeous pageantry, pageantry of a magnificence perhaps unequaled in human annals; tournaments, regattas, flotillas of gilded gondolas, processions of scarlet-robed senators and white-clad ambassadors, and parades of white horses draped with gold braid and white taffeta.

The foundation for all this magnificence was Venice's maritime trade, particularly her trade with the East. This trade was carried on by the largest merchant fleet in the world and was protected by the world's largest navy: 300 seagoing vessels manned by 8,000 sailors, 3,000 smaller craft carrying 17,000 men, and 45 galleons crewed by another 11,000 men. The ships were constructed, fitted, and repaired in the great Arsenale of the republic, two miles of fortifications enclosing sixty acres of sheds and shipyards – unquestionably the largest single industry in the Renaissance world. Some 15,000 men labored in this navy yard, where one hundred ships could be built or repaired at a time.

Venice's supremacy on the high seas was symbolically confirmed each year on Ascension Day, when the most sumptuous pageant of all, the Marriage to the Sea, was held. On this day the doge's ceremonial barge, the huge, gilded Bucentaur, would draw away from the Riva degli Schiavoni to the accompaniment of trumpet fanfares and the chants of massed choirs. The city's chief governing body, the Council of Ten, and all the patricians and ambassadors followed in their gondolas. At the Porto di Lido, where the Adriatic joined the lagoon, the doge would stand on the stern of the glittering Bucentaur, raise a bejeweled hand, and cast a golden ring into the waters declaring, "O sea, we wed thee in sign of our true and everlasting dominion."

By 1495, the wedding of Venice to the Adriatic had become one of the most famous ceremonies in Europe. The mighty came from far and wide to witness it, and as many as five hundred gondolas and barges escorted the Bucentaur across the lagoon. The feasting went on for days. To observers like Phillipe de Commynes there seemed to be no question that Venice's dominion would be everlasting.

Successive barbarian incursions in the fifth, sixth, and seventh centuries A.D. *ultimately drove the cultured denizens of northern Italy to seek refuge in the reedy marshes of the Venetian lagoon (left). Displacing the simple fisherfolk who inhabited the mud flats, these patrician émigrés established a unique society that was to endure for more than a millennium. Indeed, by the time of the third Lombard invasion, Venice had already become a haven for thousands of mainlanders driven from their vast estates by horsemen such as the one depicted in bronze gilt at right.*

The island city's future had not always seemed so certain, however. In reality, it had taken the Venetians over one thousand years of unremitting struggle to reach their position of splendor and dominion. The early years of the republic had been marked by great heroism and sacrifice, for the first Venetians had started with nothing. They were refugees from the mainland who had fled across the lagoon to escape marauding barbarians. The islands they settled on — the detritus of three rivers — were little more than marshy sinkholes, almost uninhabitable.

The story of the birth of Venice begins with the death of Rome. Throughout the fifth, sixth, and seventh centuries, invaders from the north — first Huns, then Goths and Lombards — swarmed over the Danube frontier of the Roman Empire in successive waves. They then made their way down the Italian peninsula, defeating Roman armies, destroying Roman towns, appropriating vast territories, subjugating native populations, and eventually deposing the Roman emperor, thus putting an end to the empire of the West. During these violent incursions, Roman citizens from Concordia, Aquileia, Altinum, and what are today Padua, Verona, and Vicenza — men and women accustomed to wealth and refinement — fled the mainland for the tidal islands of the shallow Venetian lagoon, then inhabited solely by fishermen. These fishermen were described by Cassiodorus, a Roman chronicler who was an official in the Goths' court, as living "like marsh birds, in nests of reeds raised on piles, to protect themselves against the waters." From the very beginning, friction developed between the fishermen and the more sophisticated newcomers. Occasionally the Roman refugees would return to the mainland and reoccupy their abandoned villas, only to be forced back into the lagoon again by yet another foreign invasion. Fortunately for the refugees, the barbarians were poor swimmers and worse sailors, and so the lagoon formed an impregnable defense against them. Thus it was in self-defense that the detritus of humanity settled on the detritus of rivers.

The most destructive of all the barbarian invasions, the one most directly responsible for the creation of Venice, occurred in A.D. 452 when the Hunnish khan Attila, called "the Scourge of God," sacked Aquileia after having been repulsed outside the gates of Rome. The Huns, a savage central Asian people who worshiped the sword as a god, had been frustrated in their attempts to conquer the Orient by the Great Wall of China and had subsequently directed their unspent aggressive energies westward, pushing the Goths and Vandals before them. Attila had boasted, "The grass will never grow again where I have trod," and he almost made good his promise. Aquileia, one of the richest and most populous Roman cities on the Adriatic, was completely leveled by his troops, along with forty other towns in the region known as Venetia. Most of Aquileia's inhabitants either perished or were taken captive. The others took to the sea.

At first the refugees settled along the outer rim of the lonely, thirty-mile-long lagoon on what are known today as Jesolo, Heraclea, the Lido, Malamocco, and Chioggia. But these long sand reefs, separated from each other by narrow channels called *porti,* were exposed to direct attack from the Adriatic, and eventually they too had to be abandoned. The refugees settled

When the Lombards invested his mainland see, the bishop of Altinum fled with his congregation to the island of Torcello at the north end of the Venetian lagoon. There he founded the Cathedral of Santa Maria Assunta, which stands today behind the much smaller Santa Fosca (left). The austere apse of the seventh-century church shelters a number of magnificent mosaics, all added centuries later by Venetian artisans working in the Byzantine mode. From their vantage above the church's crumbling marble revetments (right) the twelve Apostles gaze down upon the high altar. Above them looms an enormous Madonna and Child, serenely floating on a nimbus of dull gold.

instead on the muddy, reed-covered islands of the Rivo Alto, well within the lagoon. It was discovered that these islands, which comprise the heart of modern Venice, had a hard clay base under the top layer of mud and reeds, one that could conceivably support large buildings. The settlers drove immense wooden piles, larches hewn from the forests of Cadore, deep into this clay base, arranging them in spiral patterns and then paving the surface with oak timbers and massive stones. On these unique foundations they built their city, which was practically invulnerable to attack because only expert navigators thoroughly acquainted with the tides and shallows of the lagoon could avoid being marooned on the mud flats or swept away by the tricky currents. To protect their islands from flooding, they erected rude barriers made of wattled vines along the Lido and other islands.

According to Burckhardt, Venice recognized itself from the beginning as "a strange and mysterious creation . . . . the fruit of a higher power than human ingenuity." The foundation of the city became the subject of many legends, one of which told of a group of dispossessed Paduans who supposedly laid the first stone on an island selected for them by God, "that they might have a sacred, inviolable asylum amid the devastations of the barbarians." Later writers, as Burckhardt observed, consistently attributed to the founders of Venice a presentiment of the future greatness of the city. Thus Antonio Sabellico, writing in the fifteenth century, has the priest who presided over the act of consecration crying to heaven: "When we hereafter attempt great things, grant us prosperity! Now we kneel before a poor altar; but if our vows are not made in vain, a hundred temples, O God, of gold and marble, shall arise to Thee."

The early years of Venice, clouded by legend and conjecture, are as hazy as the lagoon during a sirocco. However, there is something of a consensus among historians as to the authenticity and sequence of principal events. From the middle of the fifth century on, the islanders apparently engaged in an ever-expanding trade. They transported oil, wine, and corn from Istria to Ravenna and to other towns on the Adriatic coast. They caught and sold fish. They extracted and exported sea-water salt. Gradually the commercial importance of the lagoon peoples grew and it became necessary to constitute a government. In A.D. 466, fourteen years after the fall of Aquileia, the people of the twelve largest lagoon communities met to elect a tribune, or representative, from each community, and thus a town council was formed. In 568 another Lombard invasion forced thousands more to leave the mainland, and the lagoon's population suddenly doubled. Still another Lombard invasion occurred in the middle of the seventh century, compelling the bishop of Altinum to move his mainland congregation and his relics and icons to the small island of Torcello, located within the lagoon, where he founded the Cathedral of Santa Maria Assunta, the oldest evidence of the early life of the Venetians.

As might be expected, jealousies arose between the various communities of the lagoon and their chief families. By the middle of the sixth century, the Venetians had acquired a monopoly on salt and salted fish along the Adriatic coast, and fierce rivalries had developed among the principal producers, old and new.

MARIS ASTRVM·PORTA SALVTIS
PROLE MARIA LEVAT

Initially hailed as saviors, the Frankish soldiers who drove the Lombards from Italy soon proved to be oppressors rather than liberators. Having formally presented the captured Lombard strongholds to the pope — a purely diplomatic gesture recorded in the manuscript detail at left — the Franks set out to bring the rest of the peninsula to heel. On land, the heavily armed northerners were virtually invincible. At sea, however, their chain-mail suits and distinctive helmets (right) were of little avail — and the barbarians were decisively defeated by the Venetians.

There was pressure from the newcomers to augment the council; accordingly, in 584, twelve more tribunes were elected to represent the increased population. They and their colleagues swore allegiance to the Byzantine Empire, which had recently conquered the immediate mainland — with the help of the Venetians — and established a capital at nearby Ravenna.

But as the lagoon's population grew — largely as a result of seventh-century Lombard invasions — and as its trade became more prosperous and extensive, it became apparent to the tribunes that a stronger and more efficient government was needed. In 697, representatives of all the communities on the lagoon met in a *concilio generalis,* or "general council." They proclaimed Venice a republic, formally created a parliamentary body, and elected a single head of state, whom they called the *dux,* the Latin word for leader that was later corrupted to "doge" in Venice and to "duke" elsewhere. The first doge was the nobleman Paoluccio Anafesto, a resident of Heraclea. Theoretically, he was responsible to the council that elected him and he was nominally a subject of the Byzantine emperor, but he soon began exercising broad, independent powers.

Shortly after Anafesto's election, two political parties emerged: an aristocratic party, based in Heraclea and composed mostly of descendants of refugees from the mainland, that leaned toward Byzantium and wanted to make the dogeship hereditary; and a democratic party, descended from the original inhabitants of the lagoon, that aspired to free institutions and leaned toward the church and its protector, the Frankish kingdom. This latter party was championed chiefly by the people of Jesolo. Bitter strife soon developed between the two parties and the communities they represented.

The arrival of the Franks, who came to Italy as a result of a dispute between the Byzantine emperor and the pope, eventually determined the outcome of the conflict. The Byzantine monarch had broken with Pope Gregory II over the question of which images were to be venerated in the churches, whereupon the pope had appealed to the Lombard king, Liutprand, to attack the Byzantine possessions in and around Ravenna. Liutprand complied, and the Byzantine governor was forced to take refuge in Venice, which was still nominally subject to Byzantium. In time he was restored to his post by Doge Orso, a member of the Heraclean party who received as his reward a coveted imperial title.

Meanwhile, the pope had become alarmed by the spread of the Lombard power he had encouraged, and he appealed to the Franks to drive the Lombards out of Italy. Pepin III, son of Charles Martel, accepted the petition, entered the peninsula at the head of the Frankish forces, defeated the Lombards, took Ravenna, and presented the city to the pope. The final smashing of the Lombard kingdom of Italy was accomplished by Pepin's remarkable son, Charlemagne, in 774. During this campaign the Franks attempted to expel the Venetians from their mainland trading posts. In retaliation, the outraged Venetians destroyed a Frankish encampment and reaffirmed their allegiance to Byzantium.

By 774, however, the pro-Frank democratic party had grown quite strong, and at meetings of the lagoon assembly it energetically opposed the aristocratic party's continuing association with Constantinople. Feelings ran very high. One day the aristocratic, pro-Byzantine

So deep was the Lombards' affection for their queen Theudelinda that when her first husband died she was permitted to retain her crown and choose a second royal husband. According to the journal of Paul the Deacon, a contemporary chronicler, Theudelinda selected Agilulf, duke of Turin, for the honor. Agilulf's vigorously expansionist twenty-five-year reign is the subject of the gilded copper helmet decoration at near right, which features the enthroned king surrounded by winged victories and tribute-bearers. The jeweled cross at far right is all that remains of Agilulf's funerary crown, which was stolen in 1804, stripped of its gems, and smelted down. Happily, the silver-gilt hen and chicks seen below — possibly created on Pope Gregory I's orders as a gift for Queen Theudelinda — was spared a similar fate.

doge, Giovanni Galbaio, attacked the see of the Frankish patriarch, captured it, and hurled the bishop from the tower of his palace.

The murdered patriarch was succeeded by his equally pro-Frank nephew, Fortunatus, who assumed the leadership of the democratic party. The newly elected bishop and his allies promptly set about plotting the assassination of the doge. Their plans were quickly discovered, however, and they were compelled to take refuge at the court of the Franks. After this episode the rivalry between the two parties and the communities that supported them — Jesolo and Heraclea — intensified. Tribunes and doges lived in perpetual fear of assassination, and their fears subsided only slightly when the capital of the lagoon republic was moved south to the supposedly neutral island of Malamocco.

Meanwhile the Franks, intent on subduing all of Italy, invaded the lagoon. Their fleet, led by Charlemagne's son, soon captured Chioggia on the south rim, pushed up toward the Lido, and laid siege to the new capital at Malamocco. The Venetians, in the face of this danger, quickly moved their capital to the islands of the Rivo Alto, which lay in mid-lagoon between the Lido and the mainland. The Franks attempted to take Rivo Alto, but the wily Venetians and the strange topography of the lagoon proved to be too much for them. According to a chronicler of the battle, the Venetians lured the Frankish fleet up a narrow channel, one whose entrance would soon be blocked off by the ebbing tide. They then enticed the Frankish forces away from their ships and onto a low, sandy island where they engaged them in inconclusive combat until the

To affirm Venice's hard-won independence – from Byzantium as well as from the Franks – the second doge of the united Venetian state transferred the city's patronage from St. Theodore, a Greek saint whose symbol was the crocodile, to St. Mark, whose associations with the lagoon community were much stronger. The presence of St. Theodore is still felt in Venice, however; a marble column bearing his likeness (left) stands today in the Piazzetta, a few yards distant from another freestanding column, this one capped by the Lion of St. Mark (opposite).

tide went out and the Franks' vessels became marooned. At this point a fresh reinforcement of Venetians arrived on the scene. Using special flat-bottomed boats – prototypes of the modern gondola – they destroyed the grounded Frankish ships, picked up their fellow Venetians, and retreated from the island, leaving the Franks with no means of escape. When the tide flowed back in, engulfing the island, most of the Franks drowned.

The Venetian triumph was formalized by a treaty drawn up in 810, in which the Franks recognized the Venetians as subjects of Byzantium – although in reality their allegiance was only nominal – and conceded to them full trading rights on the Italian mainland.

The concentration of the Venetian population and government on the more protected islands of the Rivo Alto, or the Rialto as it came to be called, marked the beginning of Venice as a united state. External menace had welded the place and the people together; for the first time in three centuries the Venetians were one people. The triumph belonged to the aristocratic party, whose candidate, Agnello Partecipazio, became the first doge on the Rialto. One of his initial acts was to order the construction of a doges' palace. Later his son and successor, Doge Guistinian Partecipazio, would transfer the patronage of the city to St. Mark and order the building of a doges' chapel to enshrine the relics of the new patron.

Transferring the patronage of Venice to St. Mark was a conscious step toward unification. The former patron had been a Greek saint, Theodore, who symbolized allegiance to Byzantium, but contention between the various communities of the lagoon had naturally made it difficult for all Venetians to venerate this saint. In the evangelist Mark, the doge found a saint untarnished by Venetian rivalries. Moreover, according to legend, St. Mark had actually had a close association with the lagoon.

This legend held that St. Mark, on his way from Alexandria to preach in Aquileia, had been caught in a violent storm and had been forced to land on one of the islands of the Venetian lagoon. While he was marooned, an angel appeared to him and said, "Peace be unto thee, Mark, my apostle." This was taken as prophecy that the saint's mortal remains would find final repose in Venice despite the fact that he had returned to Alexandria and had died there.

Eight hundred years later, some Venetians trading in Alexandria crept by night into the sepulcher where St. Mark's body lay, placed the saint's remains in a basket, covered them with cabbage and swine's flesh, and smuggled them out. The swine's flesh was meant to discourage detection, since the followers of Mohammed considered the pig unclean and consequently would not go near it. On the journey back to Venice, a furious storm broke out one evening, driving the ship toward a reef. Legend has it that the vessel was about to crash when St. Mark rose, awakened the captain, and warned him of the danger, which was quickly averted. The remainder of the journey was accomplished without mishap, and St. Mark found the peace that had long ago been promised him.

After the building of the chapel to house the saint's remains, the anniversary of St. Mark's interment in Venice became a very special civic occasion for the city's marriageable girls. Carrying their dowries with them, they went to the Church of San Pietro di Castello, which stood on a little island at the east end of the city, for a ceremony of formal betrothal to their lovers. On St. Mark's Day in 944, pirates from Trieste forced their way into the church during the ceremony, captured the brides and their dowries, and dragged them back to their boats. The doge immediately called the people to arms, and the avengers set out in pursuit, overtook the pirates, defeated them, and returned in triumph with the brides and their dowries. To commemorate the rape and rescue of the brides of St. Mark, subsequent doges went in state to the Church of Santa Maria Formosa on the day of the Purification of the Virgin. There twelve girls, whose families were too impoverished to be able to provide them with adequate dowries, were dowered by the community.

The Doges' Chapel, which protected the relics of St. Mark, was begun in 830 — and was destroyed by fire in 976 as a protest against the then-reigning doge's attempted suppression of the city's council of representatives. Two years later a new church was begun, also Romanesque-Byzantine style. That structure was destined to become, three centuries later, the great Basilica of St. Mark. By this time the city had adopted as its emblem a winged lion — symbol of St. Mark — gripping a book bearing the inscription *Pax Tibi Marce Evangelista Mea.* During succeeding centuries, the Lion of St. Mark was to become ubiquitous in Venice; it was displayed on everything from the Doges' Palace and the Arsenale to the handles of daggers and the covers of prayer books.

Throughout the violent, chaotic tenth century most of Europe suffered from acute economic and cultural stagnation and mindless political turmoil. Even Charle-

The "pious theft" of the body of St. Mark — and its subsequent transfer from Alexandria to Venice — is the subject of the tempera painting at right, which was executed in 1345 by Paolo Veneziano, the first major personality in Venetian painting. His work, which reflects the strong Byzantine influence of the period, illustrates the risen saint's miraculous appearance at a particularly perilous moment during the sea voyage from Egypt to Venice.

magne's once-powerful and enlightened empire fell apart. Venice was an exception to the rule, however. During this so-called dark age, the lagoon city expanded to cover all islands of the Rivo Alto, Venetian trade increased dramatically, architecture flowered as in nowhere else in Europe, trading posts on the mainland proliferated, and a few noble merchant families began accumulating large fortunes that made them the first real capitalists of the post-Roman world.

These aristocratic capitalists — unique in Europe, for the nobles of northern Europe disdained trade and commerce — inevitably clashed with the doges, who had come to wield near-absolute power. (Indeed, three ducal families — the Partecipazi, the Candiani, and the Orseoli — had tried to make the dogeship into an hereditary sovereignty. Each attempt was vigorously resisted, not by the people, but by the new-moneyed aristocracy.) In time, the wealthy aristocrats formed a sort of clique, one that sought to draw more and more political power away from the doges and confer it upon themselves. The foundation was thus laid for the gradual ascendance of the Venetian aristocracy, a process that was to see these wealthy patricians become, for a while, the most powerful body of men in Europe.

During the last decade of the tenth century the doge still held enormous power, however, and the times were so perilous that even the aristocrats were thankful he did. For years the Narentines, a Dalmatian people, had been sailing across the Adriatic and raiding the islands of the Venetian lagoon, plundering, killing, destroying. The threat eventually became so great that the doge, who exercised almost total control over defense and foreign policy, was forced to create an armed navy. But even a navy proved unable to fully protect the city from piracy, for the wealth of Venice had already become legendary in the Adriatic, and the less prosperous wanted a share of it.

By the year 997, the raids had become so frequent and so destructive that Doge Pietro Orseolo II determined to put an end to them once and for all by attacking the raiders' strongholds on the Dalmatian coast. In personal command of the Venetian fleet, Orseolo stormed and captured the strongholds of Curzola and Lagosta, forts perched on seemingly inaccessible crags, and soon obtained full control over the coasts of Dalmatia and Croatia. Returning to Venice in triumph, the warrior-doge awarded himself a resounding new title, duke of Dalmatia and Croatia, which was subsequently recognized by the German and Byzantine emperors. The Adriatic had become a Venetian lake. To commemorate his victory, Doge Orseolo sailed forth on Ascension Day of the following year, stayed his galleon near one of the channels joining the lagoon to the Adriatic, and poured a libation on the waters in the first Marriage to the Sea ceremony. The union thus solemnized was to last more than seven centuries.

Two years later, in the year 1000, the most powerful sovereign in Europe, the Holy Roman emperor Otto III, journeyed to Venice and met Doge Orseolo — now styled Orseolo the Magnificent — in his sumptuous new palace. After several days of negotiations the doge obtained important commercial concessions from the emperor, along with new fame and vastly increased prestige. The improbable republic, founded by dispossessed refugees on uninhabitable islands, had been accepted as one of the great European powers.

II

Bride of the Sea

In symbolically marrying the Adriatic, Venice formally acknowledged both her dependence upon the sea and her domination over it. The challenge of the eleventh and twelfth centuries was to perpetuate her new sovereignty and, if possible, enlarge it. At the time, the republic had three great rivals on the high seas — Byzantium, Genoa, and Islam — and the most annoying of these was Islam. The Moslems had conquered most of the Middle East and North Africa by the 750's, and their fleets, both official and piratical, were the scourge of Christendom. The pious Christians of the West were outraged by the Moslems' occupation and supposed desecration of sacred shrines in the Holy Land. The Venetians were equally galled by the Moslems' unabashed piracy and their stranglehold on both trade routes and markets.

The devout of Western Europe were determined to drive the infidels out of the Holy Land, and in 1095 they organized the First Crusade to achieve that goal. The Venetians promptly turned this religious fervor into money, for they had the ships, officers, and crews to transport the Crusaders. Instead of attacking the Moslems directly, the Venetians leased their navy to the Crusaders and let them crush the Moslems — thus reaping a double profit. Indeed, from the First Crusade onward, the astute Venetians regularly alchemized religious enthusiasm into gold and silver. They demanded and received high rentals for their ships and crews, and in the process they acquired trading settlements in Jaffa, Chios, and Cyprus. Sidon fell to them in 1102, Acre in 1104, Tyre in 1124, and Rhodes a year later. In 1202, Doge Enrico Dandolo — destined to be a major figure in the Fourth Crusade — reconquered Zara.

The Fourth Crusade, launched by Pope Innocent III to liberate the Holy Sepulcher, proved to be the most profitable business transaction in Venetian history. The bargain between the Venetians and the Crusaders was struck immediately after Marshall of Champagne made an eloquent speech before the doge and the entire Great Council. "We are sent" he cried, "by the greatest and most powerful barons of France to implore the aid of the masters of the sea for the deliverance of Jerusalem. They have joined us to fall prostrate at your feet, nor will we rise from the ground till you have promised to avenge with us the injuries to Christ." The tumultuous shout that followed was described by a contemporary chronicler of the event as "an earthquake of approval."

Doge Dandolo, ninety-three years old and nearly blind, personally negotiated the final agreement. Venice would furnish transportation for "4,500 horses, 9,000 esquires, 4,500 knights, and 20,000 footmen with provisions for nine months." For this the republic was to receive "85,000 silver marks of Cologne," roughly $3,000,000, payable in advance. In addition she was allowed to add fifty armed galleys to the fleet at her own expense, on condition that of all conquests made on land or sea, "we shall have one half and you the other."

The time came for the Crusaders to depart, but not all 85,000 silver marks had yet been paid. Doge Dandolo therefore struck another bargain: Dalmatia had recently rebelled against Venetian rule; if the Crusaders would help him reduce Dalmatia, he would allow them to defer payment. The new terms were accepted, and the huge fleet, the largest in history up to that time, finally set sail. Brilliantly colored banners, many bear-

ing the golden Lion of St. Mark, streamed from the masts of five hundred vessels as the ships pulled away from the Riva degli Schiavoni. The air rang with trumpet blasts, and choruses of "Venite Creator Spiritus" were sung by those aboard and ashore. The doge's purple galley was at the head of the great fleet. A band of musicians blowing silver trumpets crowded the prow, while the aged doge Dandolo sat on his throne under a scarlet canopy.

Once at sea, the fleet presented an awesome spectacle. The French nobleman Geoffrey de Villehardouin, chronicler of the Crusades, described it:

> The day was bright and auspicious. The winds blew soft and favorable, as we spread our canvas before them. So glorious a sight was never seen before. Far as our gaze could reach, the sea shone with the white sails of ship and galley. Our hearts throbbed with joy and we felt that so noble an armament might achieve conquest of the whole earth.

After Dalmatia was returned to Venetian control, the leaders of the Crusade wintered at reconquered Zara, where they conferred on what to do next. Encouraged by Dandolo, they decided to attack Constantinople instead of making for the Holy Land. The capital of the Eastern Empire was a tempting prize, indeed, for a thousand years of Byzantine cupidity had filled the coffers of the city's palaces and churches to overflowing. For some time the Byzantines had been harassing the Venetians who lived in the capital and did business there. In 1171, the emperor had even gone so far as to suddenly arrest all Venetians living in the city and confiscate their goods.

At the time of the Fourth Crusade, the Venetians were still smarting from these indignities, which they felt offered a moral justification for their attack. They further justified their move by claiming that the present Eastern emperor, Alexius III, was a usurper. After all, he had blinded his brother and predecessor, Isaac Angelus, and had thrown him into a dungeon. Isaac's son Alexius IV, the legitimate heir to the throne, had joined the Crusaders at Zara — where the Venetians promptly embraced him as *their* son. The attack against Constantinople, they argued, would not be for mere gain but to restore a rightful heir to his throne.

When the great fleet finally reached the Bosporus in 1204 and drew opposite the Golden Horn, the Crusaders were dazzled by the splendor of the imperial city. Behind twelve miles of gleaming white walls, bolstered by four hundred towers, rose immense cupolas, sky-piercing bell towers, imperial palaces, and tier upon tier of houses ranged against the distant snowcapped Bithynian Alps. In the midst of it all stood the great Church of the Holy Wisdom, Hagia Sophia, largest Christian temple in the East, its immense dome gleaming in the sun. For a moment, the Crusaders lost heart — no army could hope to conquer such a mighty city — but the thought of the treasures that lay behind those walls soon renewed their resolve.

Dandolo, who was altogether blind by this time, directed the naval attack, while the French and German knights stormed the four hundred towers and the walls. The defenders were slaughtered, the emperor deposed, and young Alexius set in his place. During the sack that followed, scores of priceless "pagan" statues were destroyed — among them the Heracles of Lysippus, Helen of Troy, and Romulus and Remus — and thou-

EN VERVS FORTIS QVI FRE

Cast during Nero's reign as part of a triumphal quadriga, the bronze chargers that surmount the central portal of St. Mark's Basilica (left) reached their present vantage by a somewhat curious route. Following Constantine's victory over his rivals in the West, the horses were removed to the capital of the Eastern Empire, Constantinople. And when that city fell to the soldiers of the Fourth Crusade some nine centuries later, Nero's chariot team was carried off to Venice. In the 1300's, the horses were installed above the main portal of the great basilica — which then lacked the copious sculptural excrescences that now distinguish its façade. A fourteenth-century mosaic (right) in the leftmost portal of the basilica depicts St. Mark's unadorned entrance with the horses in place.

sands of irreplaceable manuscripts were burned. When the smoke cleared, the Crusaders loaded their ships with cargoes of silks, statues, gold, precious gems, and sacred relics. Alexius IV was subsequently deposed, and the Venetians established the Latin Empire in place of Byzantium — with Baldwin of Flanders as its emperor and Pier Morosini, scion of a Venetian patrician family, as its patriarch.

In the partition of the spoils Venice was awarded Corfu, Crete, parts of Cyprus, the Cyclades Islands, many of the Ionian and Sporades islands, parts of the Peloponnesus, the Black Sea coasts, and Anatolia. Innumerable Byzantine treasures, including four great bronze horses from the Hippodrome that had once decorated Nero's arch in Rome, also found their way to the lagoon city. The Venetians eventually placed these bronze chargers on the balcony above the main portal of St. Mark's. As for the French, they managed to collect 400,000 silver marks, or the equivalent of about $15,000,000, for their holy efforts.

On Ascension Day 1205, the year following the fall of Constantinople, Enrico Dandolo's successor sailed forth across the lagoon, escorted by officers who had taken part in the Fourth Crusade, and wedded Venice to the sea in the most splendid *sposalizio di mare* ceremony the island city had ever seen. Before casting the golden ring into the Adriatic, the new doge acknowledged the overwhelming triumph of a group of tenacious refugees who had transformed a seemingly uninhabitable lagoon into the glittering capital of a maritime republic that embraced "one quarter and half of one quarter of the Roman Empire." Venice was now all but supreme in the eastern Mediterranean; her only real trading rival was Genoa. In order to hold her new possessions, she borrowed the feudal system of the Franks, granting fiefs in the Greek islands, the Peloponnesus, and Turkey to her most powerful families on condition that they would do battle, if necessary, to hold the trade routes open for her.

One dramatic result of the Fourth Crusade was a rapid and widespread expansion of commerce, an economic boom that fed upon new sources of supply in the Levant and the increased demand for luxury goods in northern Europe. This, in turn, led to a flowering of architecture in the island city itself and to a considerable strengthening of Venice's commercial aristocracy. It also aroused the jealousy of Genoa and led, ultimately, to the Genoese wars.

In the decades following the Fourth Crusade, Venice began to assume the appearance it has today. Paving stones replaced grass in the small piazzas, or *campi;* marble bridges replaced rough wooden spans over the canals; stately marble palaces with pointed Gothic windows sprouted up alongside older wooden buildings; and St. Mark's received its incrustation of sculpture. The new Doges' Palace would soon take shape on the Piazzetta, and Gothic churches like Santa Maria Gloriosa dei Frari and Santi Giovanni e Paolo were rearing heavenward everywhere.

These last structures, the churches of I Frari and Santi Giovanni e Paolo, were built in a style known as Venetian Gothic, a variation of northern Gothic that stressed color and intimacy rather than ethereal verticality. Both were designed to favor contact between men rather than "to isolate them in ascetic shadows," as one writer observed. This was a typically Venetian

In the fourteenth century the squat, Byzantine cupolas of St. Mark's Basilica were capped with soaring outer domes of lead, giving the structure a distinctive, if cluttered, new silhouette (right). At roughly the same time, the building's exterior began to assume its markedly Oriental flavor. The talents of countless Byzantine craftsmen — and the treasures of Byzantium's sacked capital — combined to transform the once-austere basilica into a unique showcase of Eastern art in Western Europe.

characteristic, one underscored by the fact that these churches were as much meeting places and shrines of civic glory as they were places of worship. In time, both became mausoleums for Venetian notables: Titian was buried in I Frari, which he had decorated with two altarpieces, and more than twenty doges were buried in Santi Giovanni e Paolo.

The incomparable St. Mark's Basilica, on the other hand, was begun much earlier than the Fourth Crusade — perhaps as early as 978 — but it was not completed until 1275, and its decoration continued well into the eighteenth century.

The most striking thing about the great church is its pronounced Oriental flavor. This is no severe, gloomy, northern cathedral; this is a golden temple out of *The Arabian Nights*. As such, it symbolizes the city's close association with the East, Venice being unique among the Italian city-states in having its roots not so much in Roman tradition as in the Byzantine. It has been said that Venice borrowed everything from Byzantium: her handicrafts, her art, her law, her administration, her dress, her architecture. Even her music was ultimately derived from the East.

St. Mark's was in fact modeled upon an Eastern church, the Church of the Holy Apostles in Constantinople. Its shape, that of a Greek cross with equal arms, is typically High Romanesque, but its five domes, one in the center and one over each arm, have a distinctly Oriental flavor. The original brick construction was evidently quite plain, and it wasn't until after the sack of Constantinople that its elaborate decoration was added. Following the Crusaders' return, the great church became a repository and showcase for the spoils of war, and the façade took on its pronounced Oriental coloring. Glittering gold mosaics, executed by Byzantine artists, appeared in the arches above the portals and windows. (One of these depicts the "translation" — or "pious theft" — of the body of St. Mark.) These mosaics were soon surrounded by sculptures of Byzantine inspiration representing the Signs of the Zodiac, the Virtues, the Prophets, and the Beatitudes. Fanciful marble inlays, Egyptian capitals, alabaster sculptures, gilded weather vanes, and incrustations of Byzantine bas-reliefs representing palm leaves, lilies, grapes, pomegranates, birds, buds, and plumes began to cover the uneven surface. The eighth-century porphyry head of the Eastern emperor Justinian II took its place on the balcony above the portals, near the four stolen bronze horses. So loaded with sculptural excrescences did St. Mark's become that Mark Twain, with characteristic irreverence, was moved to describe it as " a great warty bug."

In *The Stones of Venice,* the most complete description of Venice ever written, influential nineteenth-century English art critic John Ruskin laid great stress on the coloring of St. Mark's. Noting that "the school of encrusted architecture is the only one in which perfect and permanent chromatic decoration is possible," Ruskin added, "The effects of St. Mark's depend not only upon the most delicate sculpture in every part, but eminently on its color also, and that the most subtle, variable, inexpressible color in the world — the color of glass, of transparent alabaster, of polished marble, and lustrous gold."

Ruskin was referring to the exterior of the basilica. The interior is not as varied, but that space is suffused

with light of varying intensity, from burnt umber to blazing solar incandescence. Here and there flashes of indigo, ruby, and emerald leap out from the profusion of gold. This interior space is divided into an atrium, a nave with two aisles and chapels crossed by a transept with aisles and more chapels, and an apse. The whole is crowned by five richly decorated domes. The dome above the atrium displays gleaming thirteenth-century mosaics representing the Creation of the World and the Fall of Man. On the pavement below, three red slabs commemorate the reconciliation between the Holy Roman emperor Frederick I, known as Barbarossa, and Pope Alexander III, effected in St. Mark's in 1177 through the mediation of Doge Sebastian Ziani — an event that further emphasized Venice's status as a world center.

Some of the most splendid mosaics in the basilica shine from the central dome of the nave, where the Ascension has been interpreted in a thirteenth-century Byzantine-Venetian style that is remarkable for its dynamic composition. There is no static medievalism in these expressive faces, swirling draperies, and nervous movements, which are three centuries ahead of their time. Of particular narrative interest are the late-thirteenth-century mosaics in the right transept depicting the finding of the body of St. Mark.

As noted, most of the original St. Mark's was destroyed by fire in 976. After the fire had burned itself out, searchers combed the rubble looking for the saint's body, but no trace of it could be found. When the basic structure of the new basilica was completed, a solemn fast was conducted and prayers were offered in hopes that the lost relics would be revealed. On June 25, 1063, as a procession moved through the recently reopened basilica, a great light suddenly shone from a pillar near the altar of St. James. Part of the masonry fell away, a hand with a ring of gold on the middle finger reached out, a "sweet fragrance filled the church," and the body of St. Mark was rediscovered. It had evidently been bricked into the wall by a careless workman.

The chief treasure of St. Mark's — and one of the most magnificent specimens of the goldsmith's art in existence — is the Pala d'Oro, or Golden Altarpiece, made by Byzantine goldsmiths in Constantinople. This dazzling work of art, composed of enamel and precious jewels set into plates of gold and silver, stands below a canopy of verd antique marble on the high altar. Before Napoleon's troops partially dismantled it in 1797, the altarpiece contained 1,300 large pearls, 400 garnets, 90 amethysts, 300 sapphires, 300 emeralds, and 15 rubies. Other spoils of Eastern conquests include the Nicopeian Madonna, a "miraculous" twelfth-century Byzantine icon said to have been painted by St. Luke.

Although most of the decoration of St. Mark's was added after the lucrative Fourth Crusade, the basilica is essentially a tenth and eleventh-century construction, and as such it belongs to the infancy of the republic. Its role in Venetian life was to weld the people together under the protective banner of St. Mark and to provide a focus for both religious and patriotic feeling, a place where Venetians could set aside their intense rivalries and animosities and momentarily become one.

The Doges' Palace, on the other hand, clearly belongs to the post-Fourth Crusade period of Venetian

Literally as well as aesthetically outshone by the glittering mosaics that surround them, the bronze doors of St. Mark's nonetheless command the visitor's attention. Their expanse is punctuated by twelfth-century embellishments such as the two designs seen at left and right.

history, to what we might call the young manhood of the republic. As the seat of Venice's government, it was not a focus of patriotic feeling but a place of contention, intrigue, and occasional despotism. Such grim deeds were perpetrated in and around the Doges' Palace that the Venetians could not look upon its deceptively delicate façade without feelings of mistrust and suspicion — and at times even horror. Among other things, the republic published its death sentences between two columns of red marble on the palace's upper arcade — and those sentences were carried out at the foot of the granite column of St. Theodore, directly in front of the palace.

The present Doges' Palace dates from the fourteenth and fifteenth centuries and incorporates in one edifice three buildings that previously stood on its site. These were the Palatium Ducis, a private fortress-residence built for the doge in the style of a Byzantine mansion and erected in the early eleventh century; the Palazzo Pubblico, seat of the Maggior Consiglio, or Great Council, the supreme parliamentary body of the republic that was formally established in 1172; and the Palazzo di Giustizia, where the law courts were located. By the dawn of the fourteenth century, these buildings had all become outmoded and Venice's government had undergone certain radical changes. In order to promote greater security and efficiency, it had become necessary to erect a new and unified seat of government. The decision to build a new Doges' Palace reflected, among other things, the expansion of commerce and the strengthening of the city's commercial aristocracy that grew out of the Fourth Crusade. Indeed, by this time commerce had become the chief occupation of both the Venetian aristocracy and the Venetian government. Everything in Venice was subordinated to commerce. Even the church had a hand in trade; it invested heavily in shipping ventures and in so doing earned huge profits, often as much as the state and the nobles.

The life of a thirteenth-century Venetian nobleman was cast in a rigid mold. While the young aristocrat was receiving his formal education he worked as an apprentice in his father's business. He also learned practical seamanship and navigation and took to the sea for brief periods of time. When he came of age, he was formally betrothed to a girl of thirteen or fourteen, one from an aristocratic family with whom the groom's parents wanted to establish a commercial or political alliance. Once married, the young couple settled down in the house of the groom's parents, a practice that made households of fifteen to twenty relatives, often spanning four generations, common. These palaces had windows of glass, real beds, and even table forks — amenities unheard of elsewhere in Europe. The offices of the family business were usually located on the ground floor, the head of the household and his wife lived on the first floor, and the others lived above.

Theirs was not a life of gilded leisure, however, despite the general prosperity. Men spent more time at work than at play, and they were constantly at the beck and call of the republic. At a moment's notice, a nobleman could be ordered on an expedition against the Moslems or appointed to some unsalaried government position that he was forbidden to refuse and from which he was forbidden to resign. When the patricians did take time out to meet socially, their gatherings were very formal. Together the gentlemen and ladies

PERETETERN ISOLISRADIAT
NERASPERNIT

In a sense, the Pala d' Oro, or Golden Altarpiece, of St. Mark's is a historical document as well as an artistic triumph, for it reflects the tastes and talents of artisans working as much as four centuries apart. Commissioned by Doge Pietro Orseolo I in 976, the altarpiece was subsequently enlarged to incorporate panels captured at Constantinople in 1204. Countless gemstones, added little more than a century later, seem to illuminate the entire work from within, bathing the central detail (near left) in suffused, honey-colored light. The Nicopeian Madonna (below), likewise encrusted with precious stones and seed pearls, is one of the most venerated of the basilica's treasures. The Madonna's severe, Byzantine features were to have a profound influence upon early Venetian art — an impact that was only partially tempered by the time that the mosaics at far left were created. These luminous thirteenth-century panels — which depict Noah and the Dove (top), a six-winged angel (center), and a view of the Flood (bottom) — are marked by a dynamism and grace that is distinctly Venetian.

Raised in marble relief over the main entrance to St. Mark's are scenes depicting the Labors of the Months — tasks familiar to every Venetian, no matter what his occupation. The panel at near right, for example, depicts the slaughtering of domestic animals. Others — left to right — feature carpenters bucking wood, shipwrights at work, and fishermen.

of noble birth in Venice formed a kind of club, a separate caste, recognizable immediately by dress and speech. There was intense class loyalty, for the Venetian aristocrats cherished their privileges and guarded them tenaciously.

One of the Venetian aristocrat's most cherished privileges was being allowed to sit in the Great Council. All male members of the Venetian aristocracy over the age of twenty were eligible. At the time of the Fourth Crusade, council membership stood at roughly 460. During the first prosperous decades of the thirteenth century many Venetian commoners were admitted to the aristocracy as a reward for outstanding military or commercial achievements, and the ranks of the Great Council grew accordingly. A large number of new aristocrats were created after Venice's great victory over the Genoese fleet at Acre in 1257, an event that gave the Venetians a temporary monopoly over trade with the Levant, and these new arrivals also took places in the Great Council. Since the situation was beginning to get out of hand, the old commercial families gradually resolved to admit no more newcomers to the ranks of the aristocracy and to restrict radically membership in the Great Council. This would secure for them an absolute monopoly on the trade with the Levant that the Fourth Crusade and the victory over the Genoese had placed in their hands. Accordingly, Doge Pietro Gradenigo, in alliance with the leading noble families, brought about the *serrata,* or "locking," of the Great Council in 1297. Henceforth no more newcomers would be admitted, and many present members were expelled.

What Doge Gradenigo actually did was to request the Quarantie, or Supreme Court, to establish a permanent, hereditary membership for the council by voting in only those aristocrats who had held seats during the past four years or whose paternal ancestors had held seats between 1172 and 1297. Those receiving twelve favorable votes became permanent members with the right to pass their membership on to their eldest sons. All others were excluded.

To make sure the exclusivity of the membership would be maintained, the heraldic officers of the republic met in 1319 to create the Libro d'Oro, or Golden Book, which was destined to be a permanent directory of the Venetian nobility. The officers were directed to enter all births, marriages, and deaths of members of the aristocracy in the book. No one who was not in the book could ever hope to sit on the Great Council or play a significant role in public affairs.

These revolutionary measures deprived the mass of Venetians of the political rights they had struggled so hard to secure over the centuries. In one high-handed stroke, the leaders of the republic had divided the populace into two great categories: those who were eligible to sit in the council and those who were not. As might have been expected, this massive disenfranchisement enraged many segments of Venetian society, particularly those aristocrats who did not receive twelve votes from the Quarantie and were consequently excluded from the council.

An abortive 1310 rebellion gave rise to a committee of public safety, and this committee gradually evolved into the Council of Ten. Chosen from the Great Council and given permanent status in 1335, this body eventually became the most feared power in the repub-

lic, known for its ruthless, uncompromising, impersonal despotism. No two members of one family could serve on the Ten at one time; membership was for a term of one year, without possibility of reelection; there was no pay; a member was not permitted to associate with foreigners; and it was a capital offense to accept a gift.

With the locking of the Great Council, the creation of the Golden Book, and the institution of the Council of Ten, the five hundred leading patrician families became secure in their political and social power and the Venetian constitution and government were definitively established. The system was destined to last more than four centuries.

At the base of the pyramid of power was the Great Council, a primarily elective body composed of all those patricians who enjoyed suffrage. It elected the doge, the senators, the Supreme Court justices, and the Council of Ten, and it often deliberated important matters of state. Next came the Senate, which was composed of sixty members elected annually from the Great Council. The Senate was the republic's chief deliberative and legislative body, and its recommendations on commerce, finance, and foreign affairs were sent up to the Ten and to the doge and his cabinets for executive decision.

During the fourteenth century the Council of Ten, next on the pyramid, dealt mostly with cases of conspiracy and espionage, but by 1400 it had absorbed many other functions of government, such as issuing orders to foreign ambassadors, enacting criminal legislation, and making certain that the other officers of the state did not step out of line. In time, the Ten would dispose of life and death matters without appeal and its three "inquisitors" would impeach judges and even overthrow doges.

The doge and his two cabinets, together with the Supreme Court justices, occupied the apex of the pyramid. One of the doge's cabinets, called the Collegio, was composed of groups of *savi,* or "wise men," twenty-six in all. Each of these groups was concerned with some aspect of Venetian life – one with the navy, another with internal affairs, and so forth. It was essentially an initiatory body, one that sent matters down to the Ten and the Senate for deliberation. The other cabinet, an executive body, was called the Serenissima Signoria and consisted of the doge, six counselors, and three judges. Judicial power was exercised by the three high courts of the Quarantie, a total of forty judges. As for the doge, he gradually became more and more of a figurehead as power passed into the hands of the Ten.

The constitutional system was, in the last analysis, an elaborate and highly refined complex of checks and balances. The overriding concern of the Venetian aristocracy was to prevent any one of its members from becoming too powerful. Thus as soon as a doge began to show signs of becoming a despot, he was swiftly cut down and replaced. In Gibbon's succinct analysis: "The aristocracy reduced the doge to a pageant and the people to a cypher."

The effectiveness of the system was tested in 1355 when the newly elected doge, Marino Falier, a seventy-two-year-old former naval commander, attempted to wrest power from the Great Council and the Council of Ten. A revolutionary organization composed of Arsenale workers, disaffected plebians, and members of the middle class was formed. The conspirators assumed

Although the franchise was restricted after 1297 to members of the Great Council, all Venetians were theoretically capable of influencing the workings of the city's government through the public denunciation of wrongdoers. Accusations dropped into the open maw of the sculpted face at right were promptly investigated by the Council of Ten, which convened in a special room at the head of the Golden Staircase (left) in the Doges' Palace.

Overleaf:

The rose and white marble façade of the Doges' Palace hovers, airy and weightless, above the Piazzetta. A felicitous fusion of Venetian Gothic and Renaissance elements, the dappled exterior of the ducal palace belies the Machiavellian natures of the men who once met within its walls.

the names of important noblemen and went through the streets molesting innocent people in an attempt to gain mass support. The conspiracy was quickly detected by the Ten, and the following day the doge was arrested, tried, and condemned to death. A day later he was beheaded on the palace staircase — on the spot where every doge took the oath of office.

The event left an indelible mark on the Venetian consciousness. The members of the Council of Ten were so shocked by their own action that they did not even record their sentence in the minutes, only the words "Let it not be written." And in the immense Hall of the Great Council in the Doges' Palace the place reserved for Falier in the gallery of ducal portraits was occupied not by a portrait but by a black square bearing the inscription "This is the place of Marino Falier, beheaded as a criminal." After the execution the body was placed in a common barge — along with the corpses of laborers, sailors, and porters — and carted away to the cemetery of the poor.

To help in detecting future conspiracies quickly, the Council of Ten installed several wall boxes in the Doges' Palace. These receptacles, one of which was shaped like a lion's head with an open mouth, were to receive unsubstantiated denunciations. By means of La Bocca di Leone — the Lion's Mouth — anyone in the city could accuse anyone he pleased of an offense against the republic. The accusation would be investigated secretly and appropriate action would be taken if necessary. Thus, although very few Venetians were allowed to vote, all were theoretically allowed to spy.

The growth of numerous interdependent government agencies, and their increasingly broad fields of operation, made larger, more unified accommodations necessary. And so it was decided to erect a palace that would house all departments of government under one roof. The palace was begun in 1309, at a time when the Gothic style was still in favor, but it was not completed until 1438, during what was for Venice the early Renaissance. Happily, the façade of the Doges' Palace displays a remarkably harmonious fusion of Byzantine, Gothic, and Renaissance styles, despite the fact that the Venetians never wholly accepted the Gothic. The essence of this style is elevation, an impression of otherworldliness. The Venetians, however, always thwarted this soaring verticality by adding numerous down-to-earth horizontals to their Gothic constructions. The Doges' Palace perfectly illustrates this Italian tendency to contain upward movement; its lovely, lacy exterior, lined with small slabs of pale rose and white marble, is broken up by two magnificent Gothic arcades of 107 columns — 36 below and 71 above — and 14 large, pointed windows. The lower arcade is very squat — its columns are too short and thick to merit Gothic arches — while the upper arcade has taller, slimmer columns displaying genuine Gothic elevation. Any pronounced thrust that these columns may donate to the design is countered by three strongly defined horizontals, one above the lower arcade, one above the upper arcade, and one at the top of the building under the coping. And yet thanks to the rows of Byzantine spires along the edge of the roof these horizontals do not weigh the building down. Seen from the lagoon, the palace almost looks as if it could float.

With the completion of the new Doges' Palace, chambers for the Collegio, the Serenissima Signoria,

The sculptural detailing that covers the exterior of the Doges' Palace includes a number of works by Matteo Raverti, whose workshop is credited with the gargoyles atop St. Mark's. Raverti himself created The Drunkenness of Noah *(left), a limestone composition that graces the southeast corner of the palace, overlooking the Rio di Palazzo. The column capital at right, which supposedly depicts the races of man, is likewise attributed to Raverti.*

the Senate, the Council of Ten, the Council of Three, the Great Council, the electors, the Quarantie, and the doge were finally incorporated under one roof. The Most Serene Republic now had an efficient, unified seat of government worthy of its new importance, in addition to one of the most airy, graceful public buildings in the world.

The extraordinary vitality of the Venetian aristocracy during the thirteenth and fourteenth centuries expressed itself in many ways other than architectural achievement. In the realm of exploration, for instance, it was the travels recorded by the Venetian nobleman Marco Polo that, in the English poet John Masefield's words, "created Asia for the European mind." Marco Polo was born in Venice in 1254, scion of a noble family and heir to both a seat in the Great Council and extensive business interests in Constantinople. In the course of their business dealings, Marco's father, Nicolo, and his uncle Maffeo had journeyed as far east as China, where they had met the enlightened ruler of the Mongol Empire, Kublai Khan. The two Venetians were the first Europeans the khan had ever seen, and he was apparently delighted by them. Among other things, he gave them a letter for the pope in which he urged the pontiff to send "a hundred missionaries" to instruct his people in Christianity and the liberal arts.

When the Polo brothers returned to Italy they were delayed for some time in their efforts to get papal action on the khan's request. A newly elected – and tragically shortsighted – pope ultimately recruited two Dominican friars, and the party left for the Orient, this time accompanied by Nicolo Polo's young son, Marco.

Leaving Acre in 1271, the Polos and the priests proceeded to Hormuz, a port city at the mouth of the Persian Gulf. Their intention had been to proceed to China by sea, but they soon abandoned that plan and traveled northward instead. (At this point the two Dominican missionaries dropped out of the expedition and returned home.) Doggedly the Polos pushed onward, traversing Khurasan, ascending the upper Oxus River, and crossing the Pamirs to Khotan – regions that were not to be described by Europeans again until the mid-nineteenth century. From Khotan the Venetians followed the Great Silk Route across Tibet to Lop Nor on the tip of the Gobi Desert. Crossing the Gobi was an exhausting and dangerous trek for the Polos. They saw mirages, they heard strange voices, and they imagined, in that tremendous emptiness, that an oncoming caravan was an army of robbers. Finally, in 1275, they arrived at the imperial court in Ta-tu. There they were cordially received by the Great Khan, who took an immediate liking to young Marco.

Marco Polo also took a liking to China and its khan. He studied the language and customs of the country, and he was eventually given a job as a traveling administrator in remote provinces. The Polos not only held important posts in the Chinese government, they also plunged vigorously into commercial pursuits, eventually becoming enormously well-to-do and living like mandarins in a palace staffed with many servants.

The Polos remained in China for seventeen years, during which time they were the only Europeans in the country. In time, of course, the enterprise lost its novelty and began to pall, and the restless adventurers finally told the khan that they wished to return to Venice. At first the emperor refused to let them go,

but then a situation developed that enabled them to leave. The khan of Persia asked Kublai to find him a suitable wife, adding a specific request that she be delivered by ship. After some deliberation, Kublai settled upon a seventeen-year-old Chinese princess, and he reluctantly consigned her to the Venetians, who were expert mariners, for delivery to her betrothed. Their royal errand fulfilled, the three adventurers returned to Venice in 1295 after a twenty-four-year absence. They were not immediately recognized by their relatives, for in addition to having aged they wore tattered Oriental clothes and spoke their native tongue only with great difficulty. It was not until they ripped open the seams of their coats and revealed fabulous jewels in the linings that their relatives decided to acknowledge them.

Soon after the Polos' return, Venice went to war with Genoa, and the indefatigable Marco was given command of a galley in the fleet of Andrea Dandolo. The war proved to be a disaster for Venice but a blessing for posterity, for the Genoese soundly defeated the Venetians and took eight thousand prisoners, among them Marco Polo. Marco was jailed in Pisa, and while there he dictated his memoirs to a fellow prisoner.

If it had not been for intrepid Venetians such as the Polos, Renaissance Europe would have had no valid conception of the East – and if it had not been for the conflict with Genoa, Renaissance Europe might never have had Polo's appealing portrait of the Orient. Polo's incarceration was but a minor episode in the Genoese wars, however. That bitter power struggle had begun in 1204, when the sack of Constantinople had left Venice with only one serious rival in the Mediterranean: the independent maritime republic of Genoa. Determined to reign supreme over the trade routes to the East, Venice fought three bitter naval wars with Genoa. The first of these wars was marked by several Venetian victories, most notably at Acre in 1253 and at Trapani in 1264, but it ended with a Genoese triumph at Curzola in 1299, the battle during which Marco Polo was taken prisoner. The triumph was only temporary, however, for in 1353 the Venetians achieved a minor victory against the Genoese in a dispute over trading rights.

The third and decisive war began early in 1379. In that year the Byzantine emperor John Palaeologus granted the trading island of Tenedos, strategically situated at the mouth of the Dardanelles, to Venice, thereby provoking Genoa to declare war. Before long the Genoese fleet was storming the sea gates of the Venetian lagoon. The Venetian admiral, Vittore Pisani, advised against a confrontation because most of the navy was in the Levant, but he was promptly overruled by the Senate. When Pisani's fleet was all but annihilated, he was immediately thrown into prison.

Taking advantage of the situation, the Genoese admiral, Pietro Doria, sailed through the southern gates of the Lido and into the lagoon itself. For the first time since the abortive invasion by the Franks, the home islands of Venice were endangered. The Council of Ten sent envoys to Doria asking for terms, but the Genoese admiral offered none. He had come, he informed the Venetians, to bridle those bronze horses in front of St. Mark's.

As soon as they received this boast the Venetians sent a message to their admiral in the Levant, Carlo Zeno, ordering him to return to Venice immediately. Mean-

while, Pisani was released from prison and thirty galleys were hurriedly built and fitted for him to command. On December 23, 1379, Pisani and his new ships managed to slip out of the lagoon and into the Adriatic. The Genoese remained in the harbor at Chioggia, the southernmost port in the lagoon. Pisani proceeded to bottle up his foes by scuttling two stone-filled hulks in the Chioggia channel, closing the main sea gate, Porto di Lido, with a gigantic iron chain and scuttling two more stone-filled ships in the central channel, Porto di Malamocco. Pisani's fleet remained in the Adriatic awaiting reinforcements from the East. Its position was a dangerously exposed one, for the winter seas were rough and Genoese reinforcements might arrive at any minute. Everything depended upon the fleet in the Levant; if Zeno did not arrive in time, Pisani and Venice might be doomed.

Doge Andrea Contarini, who was fully aware of the dangers of the situation, confided to Pisani that if Zeno did not arrive by New Year's Day, the city of Venice would have to be abandoned and the capital of the republic moved to Crete. Miraculously, a forest of masts appeared on the eastern horizon on January 1: Zeno had arrived in time. He quickly joined Pisani's fleet, and the combined navy attacked the enemy at Chioggia. The fighting dragged on for months, but eventually the Genoese fleet was destroyed and Admiral Doria killed. The Republic of Genoa was finished as a naval power; Venice was supreme in the Mediterranean.

The Most Serene Republic might have been clearly supreme on the Mediterranean after the defeat of Genoa, but she was still a very minor power on the Italian mainland. All she owned on terra firma were the relatively inconsequential towns of Treviso and Castelfranco, both captured in 1339. At the time, Italy was a disunited patchwork of independent city-states, each trying to acquire territory at the expense of its neighbors. To the south lay the Angevin kingdom of Naples, which comprised all of Italy below Rome. The Papal States — a confederation of small principalities in the middle of the peninsula that included the city of Rome itself — were under the absolute rule of the pope. Immediately above stretched the Republic of Florence, which was dominated by the Medici family. Like Genoa, Pisa was a small independent maritime republic; Verona, Vicenza, Padua, Mantua, Ferrara, and Urbino were independent duchies ruled by despots. The most powerful state in the mainland north was the great duchy of Milan, which was controlled by the Visconti family, and which, in the late fourteenth century, was pursuing a policy of territorial expansion in all directions.

Venice needed political domination of her channels of commerce, especially the Alpine passes and the Brenta and Piave rivers. It was useless for the Most Serene Republic to import the produce of the East if she could not safely transport that produce west or north. Furthermore, Venice lacked a food supply sufficient for her needs. She had silk, brocades, gold, jewels, and glass in abundance but little meat, vegetables, or fruit. This dependence upon foreign produce had been brought home to her rather dramatically during the final war with Genoa, for while the Genoese fleet was blockading Venice by sea the Carrara family, leaders of Padua and friends of Genoa, had almost succeeded in cutting off the republic's food supply.

For many years the Rialto Bridge (left) was the only permanent span across the Grand Canal, and as such it served as both footpath and lookout. The sharp pitch of the span offered the passer-by a superb view of the bustling commercial activity along the canal, and in time it became the symbolic epicenter of the city's business district. The present marble causeway was erected in the late sixteenth century, replacing a wooden predecessor familiar to generations of Venetian merchants. The fanciful view below, which illustrated a 1400 edition of Marco Polo's memoirs, focuses upon the Piazzetta.

In 1402, Venice decided to crush the Carraras and make herself mistress of more than river mouths and muddy islands. By now she had the money, the military expertise, and the manpower to make the venture a success. Thus, beginning in 1402, Venice repeatedly stunned the Italian principalities and republics by proving herself just as capable of fighting on land as on sea. Under Doge Michele Steno, the Venetian army exterminated the detested Carrara family, conquered Padua, Vicenza, Belluno, Feltre, Rovigo, and Verona, and then struck at Milan, annexing Brescia and Bergamo. By 1408, the Most Serene Republic controlled the fertile Lombard plain, access to the Alpine passes, and the rivers that emptied into her lagoon. She had her own breadbasket and terra-firma trade routes as well as her long-standing Eastern empire. Poised upon the threshold of the Renaissance, she had the means and the security to create the first great civilization of the modern world.

III

La Serenissima

It is the mid-fifteenth century, and the Most Serene Republic is at the zenith of her powers. Immensely prosperous, universally envied, she attracts visitors from all corners of the known world. They come from Constantinople, Damascus, Alexandria, Hamburg, Paris, Amsterdam, Bruges, and London to inspect merchandise, conclude trade agreements, attend fairs, and witness incomparable civic spectacles. On feast days, when the doge is making a ceremonial appearance, the long, curving quay of the Riva degli Schiavoni, with its gaily striped *pali,* or "mooring posts," and its bobbing gondolas is crowded with patricians, soldiers, monks, sailors, traders, envoys, and porters. Exotically dressed merchants from the Levant, all wearing turbans and long, embroidered caftans, parade up and down, passing groups of scarlet-robed senators, white-robed Dominican friars, and foreign ambassadors in their brilliant ceremonial attire.

To the right, toward the island of San Giorgio, great argosies bearing treasures from both East and West sweep into the Grand Canal. Everywhere crimson banners emblazoned with the golden Lion of St. Mark are fluttering – from mastheads, flagpoles, and towers. Directly ahead a huge fleet of gondolas is escorting the doge across the lagoon in his fantastic Bucentaur. The doge is seated beneath a canopy of rose-colored silk embroidered with the gold emblem of St. Mark. Trumpets blare, drums roll, and forty-eight oarsmen from the Arsenale, clad in cloth of gold, keep time to the music. A long crimson train of damask streams from the stern, smoothing the wake. Bells are tolling. Choristers are singing. No state in Europe can match the opulence of this spectacle.

The pageantry that surrounded the doge on such occasions reflected the staggering wealth that Venetian fleets brought to the lagoon city from every corner of the civilized world. By the middle of the fifteenth century, that wealth had grown incalculably large; Venice enjoyed a virtual monopoly over trade with the East, and her navy – the largest in the world – was in absolute command of the Mediterranean sea routes.

La Serenissima's phenomenal prosperity was generated and maintained by a system that has been defined as authoritarian state capitalism. In Venice's case, where almost all wealth came from the sea, this meant that the state owned virtually everything that had to do with the sea. The state owned most of the trading galleys, the docks and shipyards, and all industries having to do with the fitting of ships. Furthermore, it owned all trading facilities – warehouses, loading equipment, and freight barges – both domestic and foreign. Private citizens actually owned only the cargoes that they bought, transported, and sold – and even these were heavily taxed by the state.

It has been said that the greatness of Venice derived from a harmonious functioning of her three great, interdependent institutions: the exchange, the church, and the government, symbolized respectively by the Rialto, St. Mark's, and the Doges' Palace. For the vast organism that was the Venetian Republic, the Rialto could be likened to its lungs, St. Mark's to its heart or affections, and the Doges' Palace to its brain. All three were necessary to the organism's survival, but if one had to be singled out above the others it would undoubtedly be the Doges' Palace. It was from this exquisite work of art that the Rialto, St. Mark's, and the

various members of the body politic were efficiently, if ruthlessly, controlled.

In reality, the government that occupied the palace was nothing less than a huge, joint-stock trading company whose primary purpose was the commercial exploitation of the East. The doge was the company's president and the Council of Ten was its board of directors; the Senate provided vice presidents and operating executives, the members of the Great Council were shareholders, and the people of Venice were all company employees.

This vast public corporation organized all major trading expeditions. Some months before a fleet was due to sail, the Venetian Senate ordered the equipping of the galleys, appointed a captain and vice captain of the fleet, arranged for the protection of each galley, and then proceeded to auction off freight space to merchants who had goods to export or who wished to order goods for the return voyage. The masters of the individual galleys were chosen from the aristocracy, and the captain of the entire fleet was always selected from one of the great Venetian families.

The Venetian government, which always presupposed the worst in everyone, never relaxed its control over its mariners. For example, when Lorenzo Contarini, captain of a trading fleet visiting England in 1402, asked to be allowed to fulfill a vow by visiting the shrine of Thomas à Becket in Canterbury, he was granted permission to do so — but only on condition that he go ashore, make his pilgrimage, and return within one day, not spending the night off his galley. The government also closely regulated the activities of its manufacturers. The secrets of Murano glass manufacture, which gave the Most Serene Republic a near monopoly on fine glassware in Europe, were jealously guarded by the Council of Ten, and glassworkers were not allowed to leave Venice or fraternize with foreigners.

Because the doges were relatively powerless, having been "reduced to a pageant" by the aristocracy, and because the Council of Ten was rather impersonal and anonymous, Venice during her great period was singularly devoid of outstanding political personalities. We can place no Venetians alongside such eminent Renaissance statesmen as Lorenzo de' Medici of Florence or Lodovico Sforza of Milan. Power in the Venetian Republic was too spread out to permit one man to acquire the stature and authority necessary for political greatness. Only in one field of human endeavor was there ample opportunity for individual genius to emerge, and that was in the field of art. No people in history ever lavished so much attention and money on artists as did the Venetians during the fifteenth and sixteenth centuries. The result of this patronage was a flowering of artistic genius unique in history.

Throughout the fifteenth century, Venetian painting and handicrafts became the wonder of the civilized world. Venetian painters became the most sought after in Europe, and Venetian household furnishings, especially textiles and glassware, came into universal demand among the wealthy and socially prominent of the age. Painting in Venice reached its maturity later than it had in Florence and central Italy, but it lasted longer than elsewhere, thriving exuberantly right through the seventeenth century, an age in which the fine arts were virtually dead in Florence and Rome.

The Venetian masters were a breed of their own.

They were separate and distinct from other Italian painters, influenced more by Byzantine mosaics and the splendor of their own surroundings than by the resurrected art of ancient Rome. Bernard Berenson, the renowned authority on Italian art, claimed that the Venetians were above all endowed with "exquisite tact in the use of color . . . supreme mastery over color." This, combined with a wonderful sense of atmosphere, light, and space, was what distinguished them most from the other Italian schools. Noting "the love of health, beauty, and joy" that Venetian art reveals, Berenson asserted that the Venetians had cultivated a love of comfort, ease, and splendor, a refinement of manner, and a humaneness of feeling that made them "the first truly modern people of Europe."

Fifteenth-century Venetian painters were concerned with a vast range of subjects, but they devoted a considerable portion of their creative energies to the depiction of a single subject: pageants. The Venetians were so fond of pageants that they demanded pictures of each event, which they were then able to enjoy in retrospect as well as in actuality. Consequently, the first great paintings of the Venetian Renaissance were pageant pictures, and foremost among them were the works of Gentile Bellini and Vittore Carpaccio, who executed some of the finest views of processions and ceremonies ever painted.

During the Italian Renaissance, painting fulfilled the same function that photography does in our century – depicting people, battles, state ceremonies, and current events – and it therefore served a practical as well as an aesthetic purpose. Painting was also imbued with an elevated moral purpose, for one of the conscious missions of the Renaissance artist was to represent ideal images of man and woman that would help maintain high standards of virtue and beauty.

The first great Venetian painters of the early Renaissance were the Bellini brothers, Gentile and Giovanni, the sons of Jacopo Bellini, who was also a painter, but not nearly as talented as his sons. The Bellinis were not aristocrats; they were of humble origin and entirely self-made. It was impossible to be a political revolutionary, or even a political individualist, in quattrocento Venice, but it was possible to be a revolutionary individualist in the arts – and the Bellinis, especially Giovanni, were true revolutionaries in their times. For centuries painting and mosaic in Venice had been dominated by Byzantine influences: figures were stiff and one dimensional, there was little attempt to depict personality, almost no perspective, and not much range of color. The Bellini brothers, like a cleansing rain, washed away five centuries of this traditionalism. In its place they introduced deep perspectives, a broad range and wonderful richness of color, and genuine characterization. And while they never lost their religious piety – both brothers spent most of their creative energies on devotional subjects – they infused new life, awareness, and drama into the religious paintings of the fifteenth century.

Gentile Bellini was principally a pageant painter, a man endowed with a deep feeling for historical grandeur. He is perhaps best known for his *Corpus Christi Procession in Piazza San Marco,* which depicts guilds, senators, and religious brotherhoods bearing banners and jeweled reliquaries through the immense square. The work is considered an extremely faithful repre-

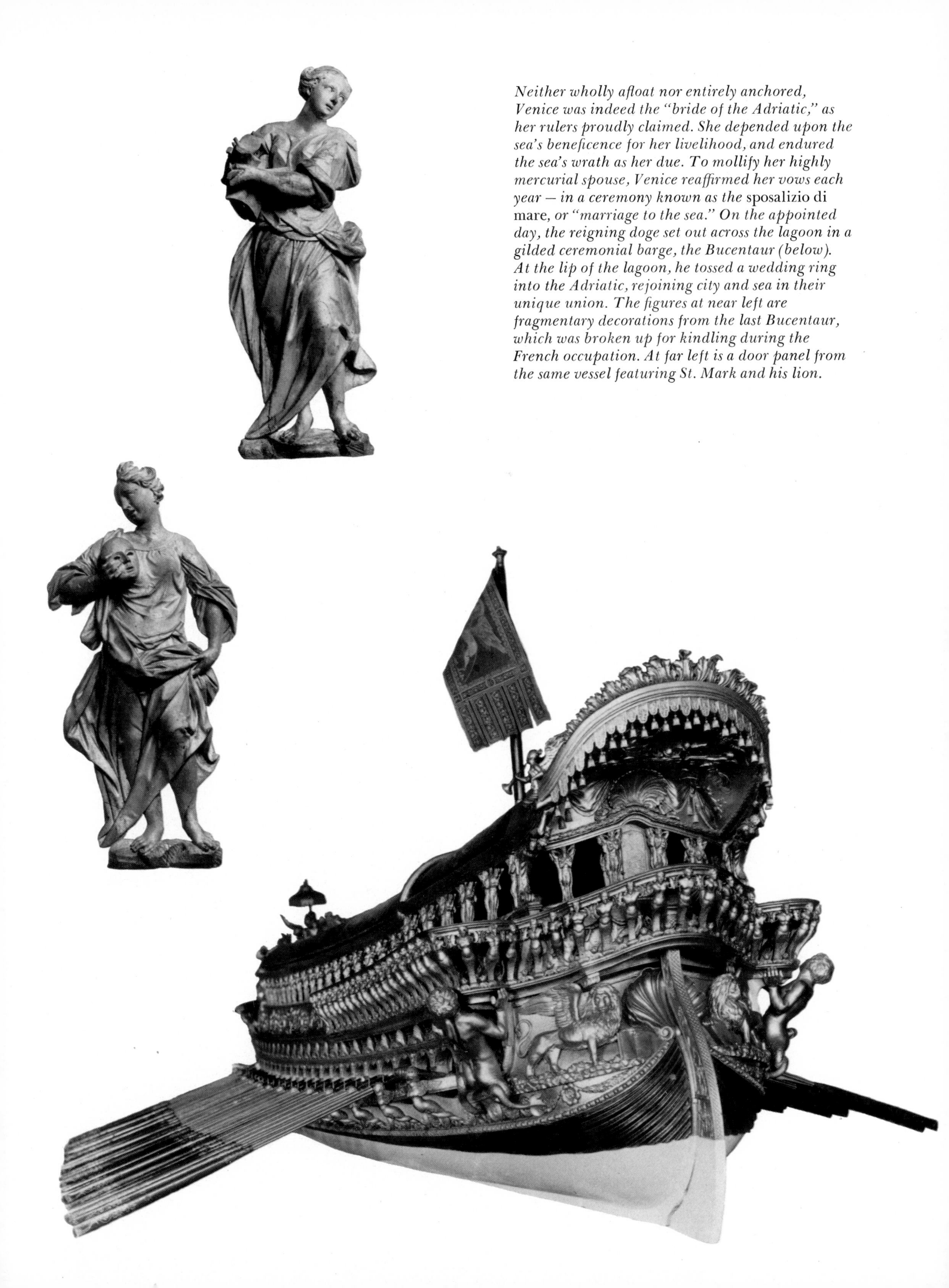

Neither wholly afloat nor entirely anchored, Venice was indeed the "bride of the Adriatic," as her rulers proudly claimed. She depended upon the sea's beneficence for her livelihood, and endured the sea's wrath as her due. To mollify her highly mercurial spouse, Venice reaffirmed her vows each year — in a ceremony known as the sposalizio di mare, *or "marriage to the sea." On the appointed day, the reigning doge set out across the lagoon in a gilded ceremonial barge, the Bucentaur (below). At the lip of the lagoon, he tossed a wedding ring into the Adriatic, rejoining city and sea in their unique union. The figures at near left are fragmentary decorations from the last Bucentaur, which was broken up for kindling during the French occupation. At far left is a door panel from the same vessel featuring St. Mark and his lion.*

It was the remarkable Bellini brothers, Gentile and Giovanni, who brought the Renaissance to Venice, dissolving the static medievalism of Byzantine art in a floodtide of rich colors, sensitive delineation, and heightened perspective. Gentile, the elder brother, was primarily a pageant painter, and his panorama of a Corpus Christi procession in Piazza San Marco (below) is acknowledged to be the most accurate depiction of the great square as it looked in the fifteenth century. The first Procuratie is visible in the right foreground, and the basilica (center rear) is adorned with its original mosaics. Gentile's works include a number of portraits as well, among them a study of Doge Giovanni Mocenigo (right) in his ducal cap, or corno. *Versatile as he was, Gentile was no match for his supremely talented younger brother, Giovanni, the first Venetian painter to work in oils. The range and facility of the younger Bellini's talent in the new medium are amply evidenced in the view of the martyred St. Sebastian seen at far left.*

Giovanni Bellini's humanizing brush gave unusual emotional depth to every portrait he produced, whether the subject was a public figure or a private citizen. To Bellini, Doge Leonardo Loredan (left) and the anonymous young man at near right were equally worthy subjects, and he applied himself to both commissions with the same discernment. For the work at far right, Bellini invited a Dominican friar to pose as St. Dominic, founder of the order.

sentation of the Piazza San Marco as it looked in the fifteenth century.

Accomplished as Gentile Bellini was, he could not approach the technical skills and depth of characterization of his brilliant younger brother, Giovanni. Giovanni Bellini was unquestionably the greatest Venetian painter of the fifteenth century. In him the devotional quality of the late Middle Ages combined with the color and vivacity of the Venetian spirit to produce paintings of extraordinary piety and luminosity. The younger Bellini, who received much direction and inspiration from his brother-in-law, the great Paduan artist Andrea Mantegna, and from the Flemish masters who visited Venice, was the first Venetian painter to work in oil, a much freer medium than the tempera used by his predecessors.

Not much is known about Giovanni Bellini's life. Giorgio Vasari, the sixteenth-century art historian, tells us that he lived to be ninety, enjoyed "a noble and dignified" existence, and painted vigorously to the end, surpassing younger painters even in his old age. (Many of his greatest works, such as the San Giobbe altarpiece, were executed while he was in his mid-eighties.) According to Vasari, he maintained a large studio with dozens of apprentices, three of whom – Giorgione, Sebastiano del Piombo, and Titian – turned out to be supreme masters themselves.

In Venice itself Bellini is best represented by his magnificent altarpieces: the triptych in I Frari; the polyptych in Santi Giovanni e Paolo; and the two "sacred conversations," *Madonna Enthroned with Saints* in the Church of San Zaccaria and *Madonna and Child with Saints* in the Accademia. There is an exalted, solemn repose in these works, "a rapt stillness," as one writer has observed, that is almost inexpressible. In the two sacred conversations, the saints grouped around the enthroned Virgin avoid each other's eyes, yet one feels that they are communicating with one another on a deep, mystical level. The melancholy luminosity which pervades these works suggests that Bellini, for all his worldly success, remained a deeply religious man to his death. It also suggests that the society that nurtured him was pervaded by a deep religious piety and reverence. The Venetians of the quattrocento may have been unbeatable money-makers, but they were also very much attached to the church and its ideals, paradoxical as that may seem.

The Bellini brothers were not the only great painters on the Venetian scene during the latter fifteenth century. During these decades of phenomenal economic prosperity, scores of excellent artists opened studios in the lagoon city, among them Cima da Conegliano and Vittore Carpaccio. Cima was born in Conegliano on the Venetian mainland in 1459 and came to Venice at the age of thirty-one. He immediately became one of Giovanni Bellini's most serious competitors, painting devotional pictures distinguished for their power of characterization and splendid coloring. Churches vied for his works, and it is said that the normally calm and dignified Bellini became quite jealous of his rival. Cima is best represented by his magnificent *Madonna of the Oranges,* a work whose luminous landscape has an intensely poetic appeal. Renaissance man, liberated from fear of nature, was discovering nature as something to be cherished and admired, and Cima was one of the first to make the discovery.

Vittore Carpaccio, on the other hand, was a typical painter of the early Renaissance and one of the very best. He was interested in both religious themes and secular ones, and his pageant paintings surpassed those of Gentile Bellini. Berenson called him "the first Italian painter of genre, of domestic life and the pursuits of the workaday world." His religious portraits were essentially portraits of attractive Venetians at their ease and, as such, present an accurate visual document of the age in which he lived.

Carpaccio painted side-by-side with Giovanni Bellini in the Doges' Palace, but all the works he executed there, together with Bellini's, were destroyed by fire in 1576. His most famous and enduring works were commissioned by the *scuole,* Venetian mutual-aid societies that looked after the aged, infirm, unemployed, and orphaned. These charitable guilds maintained meeting halls and chapels, and they commissioned artists to decorate them.

By far the most important of the works Carpaccio painted for the *scuole* is the series of paintings executed for the Scuola di Sant' Orsola. The St. Ursula cycle of eight canvases gives us a unique glimpse into the life of fifteenth-century Venice. In *St. Ursula's Dream,* for example, we see a young girl asleep in a room filled with quiet morning light. She is lying on a large, canopied, four-poster bed. The room is spacious and airy. Plants rest on the windowsills and a small white dog, one of Carpaccio's favorite subjects, lies on the floor near the saint's bed. We may assume that the picture is a faithful representation of a young, aristocratic Venetian girl's bedroom.

Carpaccio's *The Vision of St. Augustine* provides another intimate glimpse into Venetian life in the quattrocento. The real subject of this work is a Venetian scholar of the fifteenth century who is seated in his library amid beautifully bound books, objets d'art, and scientific instruments. No other Venetian artist of the time painted such scenes, and consequently we have to rely wholly on Carpaccio's vision for an idea of what fifteenth-century Venetians looked like and how they lived and worked.

After Carpaccio, the next great artist to emerge in Venice was Giorgio Barbarelli, known as Il Giorgione, the most popular of all Venetian painters and the one who had the most profound and lasting influence upon both his contemporaries and the painters who followed him. In Berenson's words, Giorgione represented a "brief moment when the Renaissance found its most perfect expression in painting." Perhaps the first romantic painter in history, Giorgione communicated a poetry whose essence was, in the last analysis, wholly mysterious. Surpassing even Giovanni Bellini in intensity of mood, Giorgione exerted an overpowering influence on his contemporary, the great Titian, that was to affect Venetian painting for generations.

Born in 1478 at Castelfranco, an old walled town about forty miles from Venice, Giorgione entered the studio of Giovanni Bellini at an early age and soon distinguished himself through his original technique. Giorgione is credited with inventing a new kind of painting: mood paintings executed on small canvases for private collectors. This was painting for pleasure, and by Giorgione's time the Venetian aristocracy could well afford such pleasures. No longer wholly devoted to making money and war, Venetian nobles had turned to

Giovanni Bellini, normally a man of considerable calm and dignity, is said to have become quite exercised over the success of his young rival, Cima da Conegliano, who arrived in Venice in 1490 and soon established himself as an artist of the first rank. Among Cima's best-known devotional works is Madonna of the Oranges *(left), which exemplifies the painter's considerable skill as a colorist.*

such pastimes as collecting art. Times had changed; soon the Venetian aristocrats would be devoting more hours to their leisure pursuits than to their work.

Giorgione died of the plague at the age of thirty-three, leaving only a dozen paintings to posterity, all masterpieces. Of these, *The Tempest* – Giorgione's famous "easel painting" – bears special mention. A partially nude woman, seated on a grassy knoll, suckles an infant. A young man stands at the opposite side of the canvas, disregarding the woman. In the background is a village of stone houses, ancient ruins, a stormy sky rent by a flash of lightning. Human beings seem secondary to nature in this unsettling, enigmatic painting. And nature appears ominous, infinitely mysterious. This is a completely new type of painting. The work has no discernible meaning; its worth is in its mood, and its mood is as elusive as the sound of harp music.

After Giorgione's early death the great and powerful of Europe fought to obtain his paintings. One of the wealthiest and most cultivated ladies of Renaissance Italy, Isabella d'Este, tried to obtain one and failed. Subsequently, scores of artists deluged the market with Giorgionesque paintings and many forgeries appeared, a sure tribute to Giorgione's genius.

While the artists of the quattrocento were adorning the churches and palaces of Venice with works destined to take their places among the greatest paintings in Western art, the city's architects adorned the canals and *campi* with palaces and churches, each patron and architect attempting to surpass his rivals in splendor and magnificence. In 1424, the façade of the Doges' Palace overlooking the Piazzetta was completed. Seventeen years later, Giovanni and Bartolomeo Buon decorated the main entrance to the palace, known as the Porta della Carta, with flamboyant Gothic ornaments – spires, pointed windows, sculptured foliage, and a statue of Doge Foscari kneeling before the Lion of St. Mark. Toward the end of the century, the Church and the Scuola of San Rocco were erected; Pietro Lombardo built the lovely Church of Santa Maria dei Miracoli; and Santi Giovanni e Paolo, destined to become the pantheon of the doges, was completed.

Along the Grand Canal sumptuous new palaces rose with the fortunes of the families that commissioned them. Between 1420 and 1434, Raverti built the dazzling Ca' d'Oro, or House of Gold, for the wealthy merchant Mario Contarini, lining parts of the arcaded Gothic façade with genuine gold leaf and surmounting the entrance to the courtyard with decoration copied from the Doges' Palace. The splendid Ca' Foscari, residence of Doge Francesco Foscari, was begun in 1452, and in the 1470's Pietro Lombardo purportedly erected the exquisite Palazzo Dario with its façade of inlaid marble disks, rosettes, and plaques.

In the realm of the minor arts and sciences, the Venetians made equally significant contributions. While the rest of Europe was living in the cramped, comfortless damp of medieval asceticism, Venetians enjoyed spacious living quarters, glass windows, silver forks, beds with real mattresses, bathrooms with genuine plumbing, and gourmet food. Venetian glassware, textiles, and household furnishings were decades ahead of their time in design and durability. And the Venetians invented the science of statistics, the graduated income tax, the floating of government securities, and modern book publishing.

Although Vittore Carpaccio's works treated rather conventional devotional subjects, his approach was far from hackneyed — and the resultant canvases are posterity's finest visual introduction to life in fifteenth-century Venice. The great cycle of paintings known collectively as the Legend of St. Ursula, for example, affords numerous glimpses into the daily life of a well-born young woman of the period. One in particular, St. Ursula's Dream *(left), intrudes upon the saint as she sleeps in an airy, sunlit, well-appointed — and altogether typical — bedroom. The detail at lower left, from another canvas in the cycle, offers a composite study of aristocratic maidens. Equally famous — and equally revealing — is Carpaccio's* The Vision of St. Augustine *(below). Once again the theme is sacred, and once again the approach is secular — recreating in intriguing detail the cluttered library of a quattrocento Venetian scholar.*

The scandal that dogged Francesco Foscari toward the end of his thirty-four-year tenure as chief magistrate of Venice hardened and embittered the aged doge, as the sculpted likeness at left reveals. Foscari's son Jacopo was repeatedly exiled during this period for supposed crimes against the state, and in 1457 the doge himself was driven from office by his political rivals, the Loredani. Retiring to Ca' Foscari (right), his imposing Gothic palace on the Grand Canal, the deposed doge died a week later.

The civilization that the Venetians created in the fifteenth century was the product of a unique combination of money, taste, and talent. Money was in superabundance largely because of Venice's monopoly on trade with the East. Taste, which is somewhat harder to explain, probably evolved through the continuity of generations of Venetian aristocracy. Each generation handed down its taste and traditions to the next, and there were no serious ruptures or cultural revolutions to challenge and eventually alter the society's fundamental style. The Venetian aristocrat acquired his superb taste from his parents, who had acquired theirs from their parents, and so forth, back to the twelfth century when the aristocracy began to assume its definitive composition. Equally important was the fact that the Venetian aristocracy not only had a monopoly on trade with the East, it also had a near monopoly on artistic patronage. The painters and architects who adorned Venice in the fourteenth and fifteenth centuries were supported almost wholly by the aristocracy and the church, and both patrons exerted a powerful influence on the artists they employed.

The third element in the composition of Venetian civilization – talent – is the most difficult to explain. How was it that this city of only 200,000 inhabitants produced so many artistic geniuses and so many highly skilled craftsmen in so short a time? We can only assume that all the conditions for the development of creative genius were favorable. There was still genuine religious faith and enthusiasm, and there was also a recent awakening to the possibilities of sensual enjoyment. There were incomparable natural surroundings. There was a society and a civilization in its ascendancy, expansive, optimistic, overflowing with vitality. And there was almost limitless money, an excess of means that, in the hands of dedicated patrons, granted gifted individuals the freedom to develop their powers.

Venice's continuing prosperity depended upon her ability to manage her empire intelligently and maintain her supremacy in the eastern Mediterranean, and until the middle of the fifteenth century she was most successful at both. Then in 1453 the republic's complacent leaders made a colossal mistake: they allowed Constantinople to be conquered by the Ottoman Turks. By midcentury the Byzantine Empire had grown weak and decadent, the Turks powerful. It was only natural, the Turkish sultan Mohammed II asserted, that the Turks should take possession of the greatest city in the East. To accomplish this objective, the sultan marshaled 14 batteries of cannon, a fleet of 320 vessels, and an army of 250,000 men outside the city walls of Constantine's once-great city.

The Byzantine emperor, who had only nine thousand men at his command, appealed to Venice, Genoa, and the papacy for aid. The response was shameful: the pope sent a small regiment of mercenaries; Genoa sent two galleys and three hundred foot soldiers; and Venice – with tragic shortsightedness – sent minimal aid and ordered the workers in one of her factories on the Bosporus to arm themselves. The Byzantine Empire had defended Europe against Asia for over a millennium; suddenly Christendom was abandoning her to the infidels. It did not take long for Mohammed II to conquer the city of Constantine. By the time the young sultan recited his first prayer in Hagia Sophia, 3,000 defenders lay dead and some 60,000 noncombatants had

One of the most technically facile and thematically enigmatic artists of the Venetian Renaissance, Giorgio Barbarelli, known as Il Giorgione, is often credited with having virtually invented mood painting. By the 1600's the growing affluence of the aristocracy had created a market for small canvases devoted to broadly secular themes — easel paintings such as Giorgione's The Tempest *(left), with its extraordinarily lyrical evocation of the northern Italian countryside, were immensely popular and extremely coveted.*

been taken captive. The male captives were condemned to a life of forced labor, and the women and children were dragged off to the harems. The consequences of this outrage were ultimately disastrous for Venice, for the fall of Constantinople had left most of the harbors, warehouses, factories, shipyards, and markets of the Levant in the hands of the Turks -- and the Turks proved to be much more difficult to deal with than the Byzantines had been.

It was inevitable that Venice would go to war with the Turks, but hostilities did not commence immediately. After the defeat of Constantinople, the Most Serene Republic sent envoys to negotiate with Mohammed II. To the astonishment of Christendom, they drew up an agreement with the sultan that allowed Venice to maintain an agent in Constantinople to guard her interests. At this stage it was clearly much more to Venice's advantage to do business with the Turks than to oppose them, but the agent soon ran into difficulties. Venetian warehouses and factories were confiscated, and in the end there was nothing to do but go to war.

Venice's first war with the Turks lasted from 1463 to 1479. La Serenissima appealed for aid against the infidel, but not one state in Italy or the rest of Europe sent as much as a ship or a soldier. It was the silent opinion of the European powers that Venice's monopoly over Eastern trade had lasted long enough, and they secretly reveled when the Venetians suffered a severe defeat at Patmos. The following year the republic lost the island of Negropont, two towns on the Peloponnesus, and Scutari in Albania.

However, the gloom that seeped into the gilded halls of the Great Council and the Council of Ten as a result of these defeats was dispelled by the acquisition of Cyprus in 1489. The king of Cyprus married a wealthy Venetian noblewoman, Caterina Cornaro, and accepted her dowry of 100,000 ducats. A year after the marriage the king died — all Europe claimed that he had been poisoned — and the island passed to Caterina and ultimately to Venice.

Three years after Venice acquired Cyprus an unexpected event occurred in the West, one that was to have disastrous consequences for the republic in the centuries to follow. Christopher Columbus, a Genoese navigator in the service of Spain, made a voyage across the Atlantic and reached a landfall in the Bahamas. Although the economic effects of this exploit were slow in making themselves felt and Venice took scant notice of the voyage at the time, the discovery of the New World was destined to divert European commerce away from the Mediterranean and raise Spain to the status of a world power — all at the expense of Venice.

Next it was Portugal's turn to deal Venice an unintentional, unexpected, delayed-action blow. In 1498, the Portuguese navigator Vasco da Gama rounded the Cape of Good Hope and reached the shores of India, thus opening a new trade route to the East that would one day break Venice's monopoly on Oriental trade and enable Portugal to rival Spain as a maritime power.

Each of these voyages would eventually undermine Venice's economy, but at the end of the fifteenth century Venice was still the most prosperous state in Italy — and although she was no longer expanding overseas, she was still expanding on the mainland. At the time, there was a good deal of controversy among the leaders

During her years of vigorous imperial expansion, Venice maintained a large standing army and a still vaster navy — both grossly disproportionate to her size. In the city's sprawling Arsenale, galleys such as the one seen on the bas-relief at left were produced in quantity for use in Venice's frequent sea duels with the Turks. On the mainland, huge mercenary armies led by condottieri, *hired field commanders, captured city after city, gradually staking out a Venetian breadbasket in northern Italy. The statue at right, dedicated to a* condottiere *named Colleoni, has been called the most perfect equestrian monument in the world.*

of the republic over whether Venice should enlarge her mainland empire or merely hold on to what she already had. In the end those who favored continued expansion, led by Doge Francesco Foscari, triumphed over the rival faction.

Francesco Foscari was elected doge in 1423 and remained in office for thirty-four stormy years, the longest ducal reign in Venetian history. He was a powerful, strong-willed man, fond of politics and pageantry, who somehow managed to convince the suspicious aristocracy that Venice's future lay on the mainland. From the time he took office to the time the Council of Ten deposed him, he embroiled the republic in a seemingly interminable series of costly wars on terra firma.

Foscari was one of the strongest personalities ever to sit on the ducal throne, and consequently he repeatedly found himself in trouble with the other nobles, who always felt more comfortable with a nonentity in office. By the end of his long reign he had made many enemies, the most notable of whom was Jacopo Loredan, whose father had sought the dogeship against Foscari — a losing cause that purportedly hastened the elder Loredan's death. Jacopo Loredan's ledger bore the entry: "The Doge Foscari: my debtor, For the death of my father." All his life Loredan waited for a chance to make Foscari pay the debt, and finally, in the last decade of the doge's reign, he got his chance.

Four of Foscari's sons had died young, victims of the plague. A fifth, Jacopo Foscari, the lone survivor, was the most important person in the doge's life. Francesco Foscari would do anything for his remaining son, even if it meant breaking the laws of the republic. On the occasion of his son's wedding, for example, he allowed the youth to accept a gift of 2,040 gold ducats and many valuable pieces of silver and gold plate from Duke Sforza of Milan — even though the doge and his family were forbidden by the Venetian constitution to receive gifts. When one of the Loredani rose to a leading position in the Council of Ten, young Foscari was accused of treasonable association with the duchy of Milan. He was tried, convicted, and sent into exile. For evidence the Ten pointed to the 2,040 gold ducats, discovered by one of their spies. Allowed to return to Venice a short time later, Jacopo Foscari again ran afoul of the Ten — he eventually died in exile on Crete. Soon afterwards Jacopo Loredan brought Doge Foscari a trumped up ultimatum from the Ten. His son had disgraced the republic and the dogeship; he must therefore resign and leave the palace in eight days. If he failed to do so, he would be impeached and all his property would be confiscated by the state. The aging doge pointed out that the constitution forbade both voluntary resignation and forced abdication, but the Ten remained inflexible. Finally Francesco Foscari yielded and left the palace. A week later he died, and Jacopo Loredan made another entry in his ledger: "Paid."

In reality, what caused Foscari's demise was not his son's disgrace but his own advocacy of mainland wars. Wars in mid-fifteenth-century Italy were fought not by citizen armies but by mercenaries who sold their services to the highest bidder. This situation suited the Venetians perfectly, for it freed Venetian aristocrats and workers alike for the more important business of making money. Among the great mercenary generals — called *condottieri* — who fought for Venice during this period were Colleoni and Gattamelata. The former led

Carpaccio, the first Italian genre painter of note, executed this view of the original Rialto Bridge in 1494. The painting's subject — a miraculous cure effected by the archbishop of Grado — seems of secondary importance; the city itself dominates the canvas. Crowded, prosperous, and bustling with commercial activity, Venice stood at the zenith of her imperial power. It would be generations before her monopoly over the Eastern trade routes could be effectively challenged, but by the turn of the century the winds of change had begun to blow. In 1494, for instance, Spain and Portugal signed a treaty dividing the New World along a longitudinal line of demarcation shown on the sixteenth-century map opposite. A vast new source of riches had been tapped, and Venice was to have no share in them.

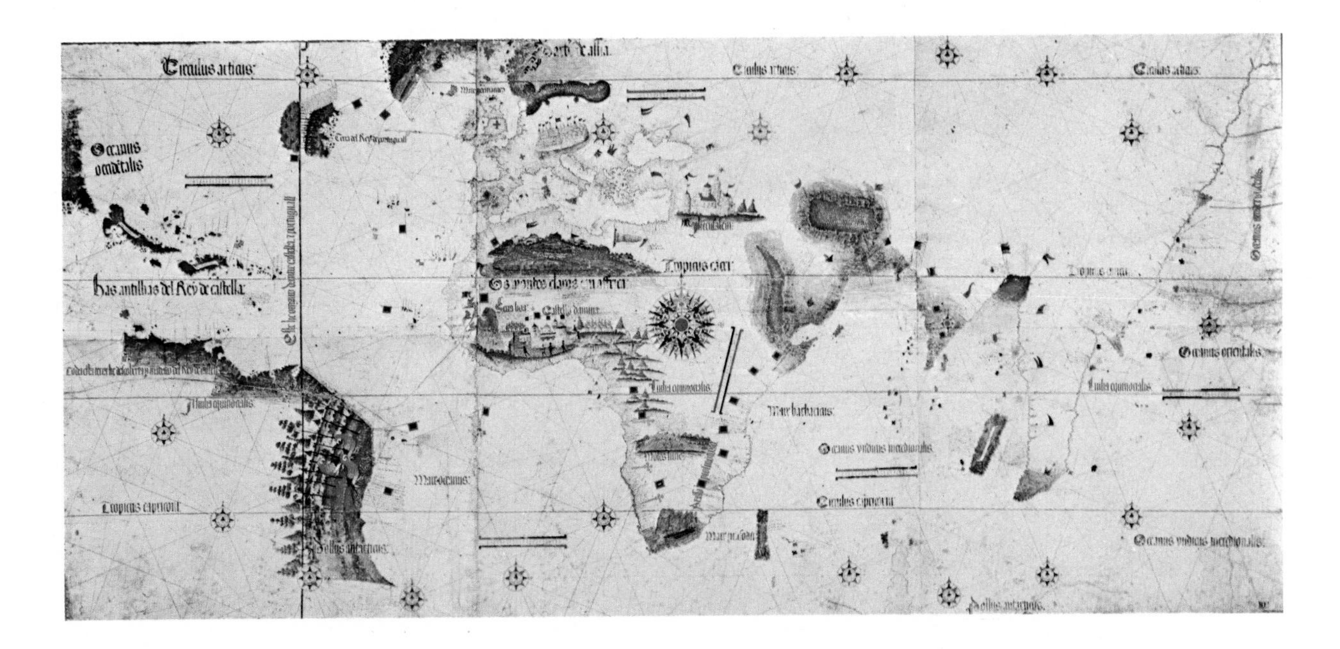

Venetian armies against Milan on two occasions – and he twice commanded the armies of Milan against Venice. (He was immortalized by the Florentine sculptor Andrea del Verrocchio, whose bronze statue of Colleoni has been called the most perfect equestrian statue in the world.) Gattamelata was best known for having executed one of the most remarkable feats in Renaissance warfare: he moved an entire flotilla of galleys and small craft over the mountains near Verona in order to transport supplies to the besieged city of Brescia on Lake Garda.

Between 1420 and 1508 Venice was never at peace on the mainland, yet hardly a drop of Venetian blood was spilled. These wars were extremely costly, however, in terms of money spent rather than lives lost. In addition to the generals, entire armies had to be paid and paid well, or else they would not fight well. But in the end Venice did gain in territory through her efforts: Friuli was conquered and annexed in 1420, Bergamo in 1454, Rovigo in 1485, and Cremona in 1499. By the turn of the century Venice, although drained financially, was unquestionably the strongest mainland power in Italy.

During the last decade and a half of Venice's expansion on the mainland, the Most Serene Republic succeeded in antagonizing every power in Italy, including the pope. She also struck fear in the courts of Europe, for as the sixteenth century dawned, the nations north of the Alps began to suspect that Venice might soon attempt to extend her power beyond the frontiers of Italy. Holy Roman Emperor Maximilian I seemed to be the most frightened of all. "Venice is conspiring the ruin of everyone!" he cried, calling upon "all people" to "put out, like a common fire, the insatiable cupidity of the Venetians and their thirst for domination." In an even more hysterical vein, the French ambassador, Louis Hélion, told Maximilian that "these Venetians deserve to be hunted down on sea and land as a people who have given up religion." He called them "crafty and malignant foxes," "mischievous goblins," "wolves," "tigers," "whales who besiege the ocean, more fearful than hurricanes or sea-monsters," and "souls midway between Christian and Turk." He told the emperor that "these Fishermen had already made plans to bridge the Don, the Rhine, the Seine, and the Rhône," and to hoist the winged Lion of St. Mark in every town in Europe.

By 1508 this widespread and irrational fear of Venice had turned to resolve, and the European powers, guided and assisted by the pope, instituted the League of Cambrai – the first alliance of nations in modern history – to prevent the further expansion of Venice. The Most Serene Republic was now opposed by no less than an array than France, Hungary, Spain, Milan, Savoy, and the formidable patron of Michelangelo, Pope Julius II. Isolated from the church as well as from the major powers of Europe, at odds with the Turks, and threatened economically by new trade routes opened up by the Spanish and the Portuguese, Venice in 1508 was clearly in trouble. However, despite these formidable foes and numerous setbacks, the republic's phenomenal prosperity was not seriously impaired. Indeed, she sailed through the sixteenth century as smoothly and efficiently as ever. It would take more than the pope, the emperor, and the League of Cambrai to sink La Serenissima.

IV

The Grand Piazza

The concept of the city as a work of art first dawned on the European consciousness during the Italian Renaissance, and no city in Italy exemplified this idea better than Venice. Throughout the sixteenth century, Venetian architects and city planners, together with several remarkably talented men imported from other Italian states, consciously strove to create a city that could justifiably be called a work of art. The result of their efforts was an incomparable masterpiece, probably the most beautiful city man has ever made.

The keystone and focal point of this unique creation was Piazza San Marco, unquestionably the most famous public square in the world. The piazza had been created in 1172 by the farsighted doge Sebastiano Ziani, who had ordered several buildings demolished to clear a larger space in front of the basilica. It was not until the sixteenth century, however, that the piazza assumed its present-day aspect. In 1517, the enormous brick Campanile – which had been rebuilt in 1329 and fitted with a marble top in 1417 – was crowned with a gleaming bronze angel. In the same year, the original offices of the procurators of St. Mark, the Procuratie Vecchie that line the north side of the square, were completed by Pietro Lombardo. The adjoining clock tower, with its two bronze giants striking the hour, had been finished in 1499. Between 1537 and 1554, the magnificent Library of St. Mark was erected opposite the Doges' Palace by the Florentine Jacopo Sansovino.

While the library, which many consider the supreme example of Renaissance architecture in Venice, was slowly taking shape, the Doges' Palace was receiving its last significant elements. Antonio Rizzo's design for a Renaissance courtyard with rounded rather than pointed arches was carried out with great success, and in 1567, Sansovino's two immense statues of Mars and Neptune, symbols of power on land and sea, were placed at the top of the main staircase – now known as the Staircase of the Giants – flanking the spot where the doges took the oath of office. Finally, in 1584, the south side of the piazza was adorned with Scamozzi and Longhena's immense Procuratie Nuove. Except for one Napoleonic addition, the Piazza San Marco has remained virtually intact since the mid-seventeenth century, eloquent testimony to the wisdom of its planners and the wealth and prestige of the Venetian Republic.

Equally eloquent testimony is offered by the Grand Canal, which is certainly as imposing as San Marco. No other avenue in Europe can compare with it in dignity and grandeur, and few would dispute Phillipe de Commynes's claim that it is "the most noble street in the world." There is something almost intimidating about the Grand Canal; its display of wealth is overpowering. Palace abuts palace, architectural masterpiece adjoins masterpiece, one after another in a steady procession for two miles. Here the greatest families of the republic erected testimonials to their successes.

Heading down the canal from the customhouse that stands watch over the southern terminus, one passes first the Palazzi Giustiniani, occupied in the nineteenth century by Giuseppe Verdi and George Eliot. Farther along, on the left, stands the lavishly decorated Palazzo Dario, Pietro Lombardo's gem built in the 1470's; opposite it, the large, neoclassical Palazzo Corner, or Ca' Grande, and the sixteenth-century Palazzo Barbaro, where Henry James was to write *The Wings of the Dove*. Then Palazzo Loredan, seat of the family that

overthrew Doge Foscari; then Longhena's massive, pillared, white marble Ca' Rezzonico with its bright blue and gold *pali,* followed by two more Giustiniani palaces. (In the second of these Richard Wagner passed the winter of 1858–59 working on the second act of *Tristan und Isolde.*) Next comes the imposing Palazzo Foscari, built by Doge Francesco Foscari, and Case dei Mocenigo, where Lord Byron resided from 1816 to 1819 (and from whose balcony one of the poet's mistresses hurled herself into the canal). Just beyond these stand three richly decorated Gothic structures: Palazzo Corner-Contarini, the rather small Palazzo Dandolo, birthplace of the blind doge who led the Fourth Crusade, and Palazzo Manin, home of the last doge of the republic.

The graceful Rialto Bridge temporarily breaks the procession just after Palazzo Manin. A single marble arch resting on 12,000 piles and containing more than twenty small shops, it was built by Antonio da Ponte in 1592. Immediately after the bridge the procession begins anew: on the right, the long *fondaco,* or warehouse-hotel, of the Germans, once decorated with the frescoes of Titian and Giorgione; the twelfth-century Ca' da Mosto, oldest residence on the waterway; and the delicately opulent Ca' d'Oro, now deprived of its gold leaf but otherwise regarded as the most beautiful Renaissance palace on the canal. Then the graceful, markedly Byzantine *fondaco* of the Turks; and a few palaces down from that, the vast, commanding Palazzo Vendramin-Calergi, where Wagner died.

The inhabitants of these great palaces were members of one of the most successful ruling classes in history, one whose privileges were great but whose duties were even greater. In reality, their lives were rigidly controlled by the state. In 1356, for example, the Council of Ten issued the Sumptuary Laws, which regulated the jewelry, table fare, dress, and even manners of every social class in Venice. Three *provveditori delle pompe,* or "supervisors of luxury," administered the Sumptuary Laws through inspectors, and they saw to it that the patricians kept personal display within certain well-defined limits. The leaders of the republic realized that envy and jealousy among members of the upper class could lead to dissension – and conceivably bring the state down.

In essence, social snobbery within the aristocracy was made illegal. If an inspector learned that a nobleman was boasting about his ancestry, he could have the man arrested and sentenced to six months imprisonment under the *piombi,* the stifling lead sheeting of the prison roof. If the aristocrat were caught a second time, he could be secretly drowned. A nobleman could only wear dark cloaks made out of Paduan cloth; if he wore a light cloak of English, Spanish, or Dutch fabric, he could be fined. A noblewoman could only wear one color at a time, and the feathers of her fan could not exceed four ducats in worth. Low-necked dresses were prohibited because they allowed room for display of jewelry. A patrician bride could have only four dresses in her trousseau, only one girdle of pearls, only two cloaks of ermine, and only one mantle of silk. Only the doge's wife, *la dogaressa,* and his daughters and granddaughters, *le dozette,* were exempt from these regulations.

Even social activities were closely regulated. One of the Sumptuary Laws limited the number of dinner parties a patrician in high office could give his relatives; another limited to forty the number of guests who could

Extending the concept of urban beautification to its logical extreme, the leading citizens of sixteenth-century Venice set about to transform the city itself into a work of art. The focus of their attentions — and the supreme by-products of their joint labors — were the city's internationally renowned public square, the Piazza San Marco, and the adjoining Piazzetta. Graceful cast-iron street lights stand sentinel upon the latter's frequently inundated paving, which is bordered along its western edge by the monumental Sansovino Library (below), the first important Renaissance building in Venice. At the southwest corner of the Piazzetta, the library abuts the old mint, which houses the Biblioteca Marciana. Its crosshatched marble floors and frescoed ceilings (opposite) tend to obscure the magnificence of the room's manuscript collection, the nucleus of which was donated by Cardinal Bessarion in the mid-fifteenth century.

Led by Il Serenissimo, the doge himself, a Palm Sunday procession moves across the piazza.

be invited to a wedding reception; and yet another decreed that at dinner parties of more than twenty guests, no oysters could be eaten. Indeed, there was practically no area of a patrician's life that was not regulated by a Sumptuary Law. Nobles were compelled to register their marriages and the births of their children in the Golden Book within a week or else suffer a fine; and if a nobleman married a commoner he automatically lost both his nobility and his seat, if he had one, in the Great Council.

These stringent regulations notwithstanding, a sixteenth-century Venetian nobleman enjoyed more leisure than his forebears, although he still had to work hard. In addition to overseeing his business — and every Venetian nobleman had a business or profession — he was expected to attend every meeting of the Great Council. The council met every day of the week including Sundays, and it convened on all holidays except St. Mark's Day. During the summer it met between eight and noon; during the winter, from noon to sunset. The Senate met every Wednesday and Saturday of the year. If a nobleman missed a meeting of the Great Council or the Senate he could be fined; if he missed several meetings without an adequate excuse he could be imprisoned.

Of all the Venetian aristocrats, the doge was the most hardworking and the most rigidly circumscribed. Il serenissimo doge of Venice, duke of Dalmatia and Croatia, duke of Treviso, Padua, Brescia, Bergamo, Cremona, and lord of a quarter and a half of a quarter the Roman Empire, was forbidden to resign, forbidden to increase his powers, forbidden to own property outside the state — forbidden to display his family crest outside the palace, open letters or mail letters outside the republic, make gifts to people who were not his relatives, go to theaters or cafes, leave Venice without permission of the Great Council, or make executive decisions about important matters of state. Furthermore, he was required to be on duty twenty-four hours a day, to give advice, receive foreign dignitaries, and make appearances at ceremonies. The only privileges he enjoyed were wearing the horn-shaped ducal hat known as the *corno,* riding in the gilded Bucentaur, appointing the bishop of St. Mark's, and holding the keys to the prison and the mint. The system was severe but it was immensely successful, for it forced the doge and the other aristocrats to give the very best of themselves to Venice, and it limited the consequences of their weaknesses.

Venetian aristocrats were very different from the Italians of the mainland, in part because they avoided the foreign domination that plagued the other states of Italy. As a consequence the Venetians developed a sense of independence — a sense of pride and self-reliance — that made them feel superior to their counterparts in Naples, Rome, and Milan. Titian's portraits of Venetian noblemen speak more eloquently than the scanty chronicles of the times, revealing men of quiet dignity, formal grace, self-confidence, and self-possession. These Venetians were serious, efficient, disciplined, dedicated, and conservative — men so accustomed to wealth and rule they had no need to express it in externals.

During the second half of the sixteenth century the life of the Venetian aristocracy moved at a more leisurely pace than it had during the heroic, ascendant

phase of their history. Venice had won its place in the sun, and it had begun to coast on its accumulated wealth and prestige. The aristocrats indulged more and more in receptions, banquets, and country life — particularly the latter. Before the conquest of terra firma, the nobles had built their summer villas on the islands of the Giudecca and Murano. But gradually vast warehouses began to spread over the Giudecca and glass factories began to cover most of Murano. Consequently, the nobles started moving to the lush green valley of the Brenta River and the rolling hills of the Cadoric Alps. There, amid some of the loveliest countryside in Italy, Andrea Palladio built the most elegant villas in the entire Western world, precise neoclassical structures surrounded by meticulously manicured gardens and groves that were destined to be imitated by eighteenth-century British aristocrats and wealthy American planters like Thomas Jefferson. Great artists, the most notable of whom were Veronese and Tiepolo, were commissioned to adorn the walls and ceilings of these country palaces with frescoes, and sculptors were invited to produce statues and fountains for the formal gardens. Before long the Venetian aristocrats had created a lush arcadia for themselves as a retreat from the cares of the Rialto, the Arsenale, and the Great Council.

Initially these retreats were used only during June and July, when the first heats began to settle over the lagoon. By the seventeenth century, however, they were frequently occupied from April or May through the end of November. And slowly, imperceptibly, the discipline and efficiency of these hardheaded merchant-noblemen began to give way to a hedonism and delight in leisurely country living that ultimately was to soften them beyond redemption and lead to their downfall.

Any grievances a Venetian nobleman of the sixteenth century might have had concerning the limitations placed upon his personal freedom by the state were more than offset by the security and satisfaction he derived from being a part of the ruling class. But what about the worker, the craftsman, the clerk — the 99 per cent of the population who had no say in public affairs? Why didn't these disenfranchised classes revolt against the aristocratic oligarchy?

The answer to this question is really quite simple, for although the lot of the lower and middle classes in sixteenth-century Venice was meager by our standards, it was the most favorable in Europe by the standards of the times. The Venetian workers were the most highly paid in Europe, and they enjoyed steady employment. The government saw to it that they had plenty of holidays, many more than the aristocrats, and it allowed them to take part regularly in the great pageants and ceremonies of state, thus giving them a feeling of participation in the affairs of the republic. Furthermore, the Council of Ten kept the prices of food and wine sufficiently low that workers could eat well without straining their budgets. Most master craftsmen owned their own homes; other workers rented apartments in tenements along the secondary canals. Thus even though the Venetian worker did not have a say in public affairs, he knew he was better off than workers elsewhere. Every Venetian male was required to serve a term in the navy or merchant marine — an experience that gave him a chance to see how the working classes lived in Constantinople, Smyrna, Alexandria, Tunis, and elsewhere. When the young mariner re-

The subjects of Vittore Carpaccio's double portrait, Due Dame Veneziane, *were once popularly held to be courtesans, although there is no particular evidence to justify such a conclusion. The surviving portion (left) of what was originally a more nearly square canvas reveals two elaborately coifed, richly dressed, and clearly disaffected Venetian matrons surrounded by their personal menagerie. Ladies of substance or ladies of leisure, they display the pervasive ennui that infected most levels of the lagoon city's highly regulated and rigidly stratified society. In sharp contrast, the alert bearing and forthright countenance of the red-hatted citizen at right — whose portrait is variously attributed to Carpaccio and to Lorenzo Lotto — reveal the sort of professional acumen that underlay the Venetian republic's commercial triumphs.*

turned to Venice he told his relatives and friends how their counterparts were living in Egypt or on the Black Sea, and they all rejoiced that they were Venetians.

Of all the workers in Venice the *arsenalòtti* were the best off and the most patriotic. They were paid their wages every day, immediately after work. They had tremendous esprit de corps, marched to and from the Arsenale like an army, and were fanatical about keeping in good physical shape, maintaining their own gymnasium within the walls of the Arsenale. The *arsenalòtti* and their co-workers did not run the same risks that the aristocrats did — another compensation for their lack of political power. If an admiral lost a battle, he was hurled into a dungeon. If an ambassador became too friendly with a foreign dignitary, he could be executed. But the courts were rarely so severe with the workers; only the highly paid master glassblowers and lacemakers ran similar risks.

Religion played an important part in the life of a Venetian worker, and all working-class families went to church regularly and participated in church festivities. Although belief in immortality declined among the patricians in the sixteenth century, it persisted among the lower classes, proving a great consolation for whatever hardships they had to bear. However, the institution most responsible for keeping the lower and middle classes content during this period was that of the *scuola,* or "guild," not the church. These confraternities of laymen were grouped according to trades — one for glassworkers, one for cobblers, one for barbers — and also according to ethnic backgrounds — one for Slavs, one for Albanians, one for Greeks. In time the *scuole* became substitutes for political activity, the members of each guild electing their own officers, paying annual dues, and voting a program for the year. Each was devoted to a particular religious cult, and each performed a particular charity: one worshiped St. Ursula, another St. George; one looked after the aged, another orphans, another the chronically sick. The *scuole* were communities within a community, and their members took great pride in them, commissioning artists such as Carpaccio and Tintoretto to decorate their meeting halls. The glassblowing, bead-making, and glass-staining guild on Murano even had its own little doge, a *podestà* appointed from a noble family. It also had its own Golden Book of 173 families, all master glassblowers belonging to what amounted to a technological nobility.

One of the most favored of the nonpatrician classes in Venice was that of the courtesans. By the end of the sixteenth century, there were some 11,600 courtesans in the lagoon city, twelve times the number of patrician wives. Their names and addresses were published in a book, copies of which may be perused today in the Library of St. Mark. They were the only commoners who mixed freely with the upper class, and many were renowned for their intelligence and wit as well as for their sexual expertise. They offered pleasures to the Venetian nobleman that his wife was either too virtuous or too inept to provide, and they were well paid for their services. But if we are to believe Carpaccio, their lot was a dreary one; there are no sadder faces in Venetian portraiture than Carpaccio's *Due Dame Veneziane,* a work popularly known as *The Courtesans.*

One of the most important minorities in sixteenth-century Venice was the Jews. They first came to Venice

as itinerant merchants, setting up businesses in the Rialto district during stopovers between one journey and another. A few merchants remained and raised families, and by the twelfth century there were some 1,300 Jews living in the lagoon area. Most of them had settled on the island of Spinalunga, later called the Giudecca. From the beginning, La Serenissima imposed strict limitations on their activities. They were forbidden to trade with Christians or follow any profession but medicine. On March 20, 1516, the Great Council decreed that all Venetian Jews would have to move to an area near San Girolamo, now known as the Ghetto, which would be surrounded by a high wall and have only two gates, both guarded by Christians. In time the Ghetto provided complete services for the five thousand members of the Jewish community: kosher butcher shops and bakeries, three banks, a hospital, and five synagogues. A number of learned Venetian Jews became professors of medicine and philosophy at the University of Padua, but their greatest contribution was in book publishing, a field in which the Venetians were in the avant-garde. The first printed editions of the Pentateuch and the Talmud were published by Daniel Bomberg's printing house in the Ghetto, and from that time on the most important Hebrew texts were first published in Venice.

Visitors to Venice in the sixteenth and seventeenth centuries never failed to be amazed at how "sweetly disposed" the population was. There were never any strikes, riots, or insurrections; aristocrats were extremely cordial to commoners, and commoners were extremely respectful of the aristocracy. In closing the Great Council and creating what amounted to a patrician caste, Doge Gradenigo had eliminated rivalry between the patricians and the commoners by making it impossible for a commoner to ascend to the patrician class. It was a social system that goes against the contemporary grain, but it clearly had its merits, for in over five hundred years the commoners never rebelled against the aristocratic oligarchy, and the public order maintained in Venice was the envy of every other major city in Western Europe.

Life in sixteenth-century Venice was, for all classes, highly disciplined. The Venetians functioned like the officers and a crew of a modern warship. Bells were tolled to wake them up, to announce the start of work, the end of work, and curfew. There were periods of relaxation, however. One of these occurred in 1574 when twenty-three-year-old King Henry III of France made a state visit to La Serenissima. Because Spain had recently conquered most of the Italian peninsula, Venice was anxious to secure France as an ally, and when the young French king came to the lagoon city the patricians pulled out all stops in their efforts to impress him. The Sumptuary Laws were suspended for ten days, enabling the women to exhibit bosoms heaped with jewels, the men to wear costly silks and brocades, and both to adorn their gondolas with gold fittings and red damask.

Henry was brought from terra firma to the city in a magnificently decorated vessel rowed by four hundred Slavic oarsmen and escorted by fourteen galleys. When he debarked in Venice, the French king encountered a huge triumphal arch erected by Palladio and decorated with paintings by Veronese and Tintoretto. He was then escorted to St. Mark's, where he was astonished

Within months of his coronation in 1574, Henry III of France paid a state visit to Venice. The young monarch's arrival (left) provided the pageant-loving Venetians with all the excuse they needed for a display of ceremonial pomp that was without equal in all of Europe. The Sumptuary Laws governing personal dress and public consumption were temporarily suspended, and an orgy of ostentation ensued. Gondolas and citizens alike were decked out in damask and gold, and an enormous triumphal arch, hung with works by Tintoretto and Veronese, was erected in the heart of the lagoon city.

to find that a vast blue awning painted with stars had been thrown over the square and the pavement had been entirely covered with gorgeous Oriental carpets.

Henry stayed at the Palazzo Foscari on the Grand Canal, in an apartment embellished with cloth of gold, carpets from the East, rare marbles, silks, velvets, and porphyries. His bedsheets were of crimson silk, and the pictures hanging on the walls were by Giovanni Bellini, Titian, Veronese, and Tintoretto. A welcome banquet to which three thousand guests were invited was held in the vast Hall of the Great Council in the Doges' Palace. Seated under a golden canopy, the king chose from twelve hundred different dishes and three hundred different kinds of sweets. The feast was served on gold and silver plate worth 200,000 crowns, and the table was decorated with spun-sugar figures of popes, doges, and gods.

During Henry's ten-day stay, sea pageants and regattas were held each afternoon. Sea monsters made of Murano glass and mounted on barges belched clouds of smoke and flame as the festivities unfolded, and by the time it was all over the king, whose normal practice was to walk about strange cities incognito, was utterly satiated. It was said that Henry never recovered from Venice; after La Serenissima, the rest of the world seemed shabby. In the end, Venice got what she wanted – an ally against Spain and a reputation for sumptuous living that soon made her the pleasure mecca of Europe.

While the patricians of sixteenth-century Venice were raising monuments to their prosperity along the canals of the city and the valleys of the Brenta and Cadore, and while the middle classes were erecting more *scuole* and the bishops were erecting more churches, artists labored in their *bottege* producing paintings for all three patrons.

Foremost among them was the great Titian, whose patrons included not only patricians, *scuole,* and bishops, but also kings, popes, and emperors. Titian belongs to the High Renaissance, a time when the styles that had originated in the previous century were perfected and brought to their maximum development. In fact, Titian's long life – 1477 to 1576 – spanned the entire range of Renaissance painting in Venice; he personally knew his predecessors Giovanni and Gentile Bellini and Vittore Carpaccio, as well as his successors Veronese and Tintoretto – and he profited from all of them. Born at Preve di Cadere in Venetia in 1477, Titian was sent to Venice to study under Giovanni Bellini at the age of ten. He soon began to imitate the style of his fellow apprentice, Giorgione, who was evidently the star of Bellini's studio, and after Giorgione died Titian inherited his place as the leading Venetian artist. At the age of twenty-three he produced one of the greatest masterpieces of Venetian painting, *The Assumption of the Virgin* in I Frari. His portrait of Frederick Barbarossa kneeling before Pope Alexander III, executed shortly thereafter for the Hall of the Great Council, netted Titian a permanent appointment from the Venetian Republic – with an annual stipend of three hundred crowns – to paint the portrait of each newly elected doge. By then commissions were pouring into Titian's studio: he painted the patriarchs of the Grimani and Loredan families, and he finished a portrait of Francis I of France. Titian also painted Philip II of Spain, from whom he received a life annuity of two hundred crowns.

The contemporaries who vied for his services came to call Titian "the donor of immortality," a well-justified tribute to the artist's powers of characterization. As the portrait at left of Andrea Gritti confirms, the designation was apt: the saturnine doge's countenance is as arresting today as it was four centuries ago. The Gritti portrait is but one of hundreds that Titian completed during a lifetime that spanned the entire range of Renaissance painting in Venice. Remarkably enough, the artist produced one of his most acclaimed canvases, The Assumption of the Virgin, *which hangs above the high altar in the Church of I Frari (right), at the age of twenty-three — some three quarters of a century before his death.*

Titian had won an international reputation as "the donor of immortality," and the princes of Europe — who had grown skeptical about the possibility of life after death — clamored for his brush, which they felt would assure their survival in the centuries to come. Vasari tells us that the annuity granted by Philip II, combined with others, gave Titian an annual lifetime income of seven hundred crowns, irrespective of what he received for his paintings.

In time Titian became an extremely wealthy man, living with his family in the sumptuous Palazzo Barbarigo on the Grand Canal. Vasari noted that the most famous Venetian of his day had "always been healthy and happy" and that he had "received from heaven only blessings and favors." He observed that every distinguished man visiting Venice sought Titian out, adding: "To say nothing of his excellence in art, he has always distinguished himself by courtesy, goodness, and rectitude."

Titian's art was exceedingly representative of the tastes and attitudes of his age. In the sixteenth century men began to awaken to their uniqueness as individuals, and Titian responded to this new self-consciousness with some of the most psychologically penetrating portraits in all art. It was also an age that was awakening to a new joy in the senses, to a hedonism long suppressed, and Titian responded by filling canvases with bacchanals, *fêtes champêtres,* and naked female flesh. It was a worldly age, one in which the Christian religion was beginning to exert less and less influence, and Titian responded to this shift with scenes of court life, episodes from classical mythology, and allegories of Neoplatonic significance.

Titian is appreciated most for the richness of his color, the amplitude and depth of his space, the power of his characterization, and his sense of drama — qualities present even in such early works as *The Assumption of the Virgin.* Given the power of Titian's art, it is unfortunate that he never turned his genius toward depicting his own city, as Gentile Bellini and Carpaccio had done, and as Canaletto and Guardi were to do in the future. The Roman satirist Pietro Aretino, for one, felt the lack. Describing the view from his window on the Grand Canal, he wrote:

> The air was such as an artist would like to depict who grieved that he was not Titian. The stonework of the houses, though solid, seemed artificial, the atmosphere varied from clear to leaden. The clouds above the roofs merged into a distance of smokey grey, the nearest blazing like suns, more distant ones glowing as molten lead dissolving at last into horizontal streaks, now greenish blue, now bluish green, cutting the palaces as they cut them in the landscapes of Vecelli. And as I watched the scene I exclaimed more than once, "O Titian, where art thou, and why not here to realize the scene?"

Titian's immediate successor was Jacopo Robusti, known as Il Tintoretto, an artist so different in temperament, outlook, and style as to be Titian's antithesis. He was born in 1518 into a humble family, the son of a *tintor,* or "dyer" — and hence his nickname, which means "the little dyer." Very little is known about Tintoretto's life, although it is thought that he became an apprentice in his father's *tintoria* at an early age. He soon showed more of an aptitude for painting than dyeing, however, and was sent to an artist's studio.

Tintoretto, Titian's successor as dean of Venetian painters, was an artist of immense energy and intense spirituality whose works display a fervor uncharacteristic of the serene late Renaissance. Scores of Tintoretto's canvases still hang in Venice, among them the enormous Paradiso, *which covers one entire wall in the vast Hall of the Great Council in the Doges' Palace. The eighteenth-century view at left, which depicts a plenary session of the council, includes not only Tintoretto's panoramic work but also Veronese's* The Apotheosis of Venice, *set into an oval frame in the ceiling. Attendance at council sessions was mandatory for Venetian senators such as the one at right, whose portrait is attributed to the indefatigable Tintoretto.*

Throughout his long life he remained essentially bourgeois, a hardworking paterfamilias devoted to his wife and children.

Unlike Titian, Tintoretto did not move in cosmopolitan circles, and he left Venice only once before his death in 1594. Having very few princely patrons, he was not nearly as prosperous as Titian. His outlook was singularly unworldly despite the luxury-loving times, and it might almost be said that he embodied an intense, medieval spirituality in Renaissance forms. Whereas Titian rendered the divine in strictly human terms, Tintoretto's religious subjects always had a mystical, supernatural aura to them, one that led Henry James to observe that every line Tintoretto drew had moral conviction behind it.

To understand the powerful, disquieting art of Tintoretto we must briefly consider the age in which he lived. Almost all of Italy had fallen under the domination of Spain; northern Europe was in open revolt against the Catholic church; and the humanists of Florence and Rome, once so optimistic, were beginning to lose their great faith in man. Concurrently, Venice was beginning to experience her first serious financial and political reverses, and the papacy was instituting the Counter-Reformation in an effort to combat Protestantism. A pall of censorship and political oppression was spreading across Italy, and Venice, although more independent than the other Italian states, was not entirely immune to it.

Tintoretto must have felt the new spiritual climate intensely, for there is little Renaissance repose in his work – none of Giovanni Bellini's quiet solemnity, none of Titian's courtly dignity. Like Michelangelo, a primary influence on his art, Tintoretto had a great capacity for work, painting on an epic scale and displaying almost superhuman energy. There is a passionate intensity and a power of imagination in his painting lacking in the works of Bellini, Giorgione, and Titian – so much so that Tintoretto often seems to be a man possessed, consumed with mystical visions of redemption and damnation. He frequently floods his canvases with an eerie, phantasmagoric light, and he indulges in scenes of atrocious suffering and savage, primordial violence.

There are relatively few works of Titian's in Venice despite his enormous output, but there are scores and scores of Tintorettos, fifty of them in the Scuola and Church of San Rocco alone. The great cycle in the Scuòla di San Rocco occupied Tintoretto for twenty-three years, making it the most sustained effort of creation in all art.

The artist's labors began in 1564, the year that the Scuola di San Rocco, whose particular charity was caring for victims of plagues, established a competition for the decoration of their *sala dell'albergo,* or "meeting hall." While Veronese, Salviati, and Zuccaro worked up designs for the decoration, Tintoretto painted an entire panel and had it secretly installed and veiled. On the day of judgment, when the confraternity's officers assembled in the hall to look over the designs, Tintoretto arrived, pulled a string, and unveiled his completed work, offering it as a gift to the *scuola.* It did not take long for the confraternity to make up its mind; an agreement was drawn up with Tintoretto whereby he agreed to decorate all of San Rocco, producing no less than three paintings a year. If in the

Five years after he emigrated to Venice from the mainland, Paolo Veronese was awarded a commission that established him as a worthy successor to Titian and Tintoretto. Charged with decorating the Barbaro family's superb terra firma villa at Maser (right), Veronese produced a series of delicate trompe l'oeil frescoes that softened and complemented Andrea Palladio's rigidly symmetrical design. The artist's truly lighthearted manner, evident in the details seen at left, precisely captured the contemporary Venetian mood.

course of his work he became too infirm to paint, he would receive an annual annuity of one hundred ducats for the rest of his life.

Violence — a theme not usually associated with Venetian art — plays a major role in many of Tintoretto's canvases. These include depictions of St. Lawrence being burned alive on a gridiron, Cain murdering Abel, and a grotesque *Massacre of the Innocents* — each of which inflicts the most gruesome details upon the viewer. We note in these disturbing works that the artist frequently abandons positive primary colors — so popular in the early Renaissance — and resorts to the use of discordant tonalities and colors of negative effect: purples, browns, blacks, and olives.

Tintoretto was a controversial figure in his day, and he has become even more controversial since his death. Pietro Aretino considered him a genius, but Vasari called him "extravagant" and "capricious. . . . the most terrifying and impossible brain painting has ever had." At his best, Tintoretto was powerfully dramatic and convincing; at his worst, he was manneristic and histrionic. But no one can deny him energy, and if we are looking for a hint of the energy that the common people of Venice had at the time of their greatness we need only look at the works of Il Tintoretto. Henry James wrote of Tintoretto's self-portrait, painted in old age, that it portrayed "a man who felt he had given the world more than the world was likely to repay." The same might be said of Venice today.

If Tintoretto was not a typical representative of the Venetian spirit, his contemporary Paolo Veronese certainly was. In Veronese the Most Serene Republic found its supreme glorifier, a radiant, joyful artist who seemed to be immune to the ominous presence of Spain, the atmosphere of guilt and repression generated by the Counter-Reformation, the disillusionment of the humanists, the empty warehouses on the Rialto — everything, in fact, that Tintoretto was so obviously aware of and that the rest of Venice so obviously wanted to forget.

Shortly after he arrived in Venice in 1555, Veronese was engaged by the state to decorate the Doges' Palace and by the church to do a series of frescoes for the Church of San Sebastiano, commissions that were to occupy him intermittently for many years. At the same time he completed some frescoes for the Library of St. Mark that won him the admiration of Titian, a prize of a gold necklace, and greatly increased recognition in his adopted city. Then in 1560 he was awarded a job that was to propel him into the first rank of Venetian artists. The director of the Arsenale, Marcantonio Barbaro, commissioned him to decorate the magnificent villa that Andrea Palladio had built for the Barbaro family at Maser, and the resulting frescoes were so well received that Veronese came into tremendous demand. The friars of Palladio's San Giorgio Maggiore persuaded him to paint a Last Supper for their refectory, and later the Dominican friars of Santi Giovanni e Paolo commissioned him to do a Last Supper for *their* refectory, to take the place of the Titian *Last Supper* that was destroyed by fire in 1571. Veronese's *Last Supper,* a lavish banquet, was condemned by the church as "indecent and irreverent" and earned the artist a trial before the Inquisition.

In contrast to Tintoretto, Veronese was unfailingly radiant, sunny, serene, and joyful — an artist com-

mitted to ideals of physical beauty, human triumph, and material splendor. He was gifted with a poetic imagination and extraordinary powers as a colorist, and he was an incomparable master of trompe l'oeil.

To appreciate Veronese's powers as a master of ceiling decoration we need go no further than the Doges' Palace. There, glowing amid immense gold frames, we behold his luminous tributes to his adopted city. The ceiling of the Hall of the Council of Ten, for example, is dominated by *Juno Raining Her Gifts on Venice,* a dazzling work that depicts the goddess pouring golden coins, jewels, crowns, and the ducal *corno* upon an allegorical figure of La Serenissima. In the Hall of the Great Council, occupying the huge gold oval at the head of the chamber, is *The Apotheosis of Venice,* a painting so sumptuous, so happy, and so triumphant as to defy literal description. Henry James came as close as anyone to conveying the effect of this work in his *Italian Hours:*

> He swims before you in a silver cloud; the thrones in an eternal morning. The deep blue sky burns behind him, streaked across with milky bars; the white colonnades sustain the richest canopies, under which the first ladies and gentlemen in the world both render homage and receive it. Their glorious garments rustle in the air of the sea and their sunlighted faces are the very complexion of Venice. . . . Never was a painter more nobly joyous, never did an artist take a greater delight in life, seeing it all as a kind of breezy festival and feeling it through the medium of perpetual success. He revels in the gold-framed ovals of the ceilings, multiplies himself there with the fluttering movement of an embroidered banner that tosses itself into the blue. He was the happiest of painters, and produced the happiest picture in the world.

In the Villa Barbaro at Maser one may enjoy Veronese in another vein, as the decorative illusionist par excellence. Here is a doorway with a servant about to walk through it; here are windows with children peering through them; here is the lady of the house, the Countess Giustiniani-Barbaro, standing on a balcony with her children's nurse, a child, a parrot, and a dog. The scenes are so palpable they seem to be real. For the next two centuries Venetian artists were to imitate Veronese's technique, but none, with the possible exception of Tiepolo, with as much success.

Paolo Veronese was the last great painter of the Venetian Renaissance; after his death the art of painting in Venice gradually, but inexorably, declined. During the long sunset of the republic, Venice produced two good landscape painters, Canaletto and Guardi; a minor master of genre paintings, Pietro Longhi; one genius of frescoe, Giovanni Battista Tiepolo – and after that, silence. But that is another story. In sixteenth-century Venice the arts were still very much alive. Besides giving the world three of the greatest painters of all time, the Most Serene Republic also produced an architect of consummate genius during the late sixteenth century, Andrea Palladio.

Apprenticed at the age of sixteen to a stonemason in Vicenza from whom he learned the rudiments of architecture, this remarkably talented Paduan soon caught the attention of local humanists and art patrons. His first patron, Gian Giorgio Trissino, who nicknamed him "Palladio" after Pallas, the goddess of wisdom, took him to Rome, where the budding architect studied

"We painters use the same license as poets and madmen," Veronese informed the Inquisition — and he steadfastly refused to alter his Last Supper *(below) to conform with church dictates of propriety in the depiction of sacred scenes. Instead, the artist changed the name of his work to* The Feast in the House of Levi, *retaining the dwarfs, parrots, dogs, jesters, and other peripheral figures that had aroused the Inquisitors' ire. Far from ridiculing the church, Veronese's work reaffirmed the spirit of the late Renaissance, which embraced pageantry with little regard for asceticism.*

the work of Marcus Vitruvius Pollio, a Roman architect of the first century B.C., and the remains of classical architecture, influences that were to determine the future course of his career. For when he reached maturity, Palladio developed a style that was essentially an adaptation of ancient Roman architecture to the ambience of Venetia and the needs of Venetian noblemen and ecclesiastics. In this spirit he placed Roman temple porticoes on the façades of villas and churches, and turning his back on Gothic irregularity, designed buildings in accordance with strict rules of symmetry derived ultimately from the theories of Vitruvius. In the process Palladio created architectural surroundings that, in Berenson's word, "vitalize" us.

Standing in a Palladian building, whether it be a villa, a palace, or a church, we feel enlarged and liberated. The space is never overwhelming, the various elements of the design are always in perfect harmony with one another, and there is always an abundance of light. The architect's most famous rule was: "A town should be nothing but a big house, and a house should be nothing but a small town." And Palladio's "houses," if one can call his elegant villas that, do contain everything an ideal town should have — theaters, granaries, stores, chapels, miniature piazzas, gardens, parks, fountains, pools, greenhouses, and apartments.

In Venice Palladio is represented by two masterpieces of ecclesiastical architecture, San Giorgio Maggiore on the island of San Giorgio opposite the Doges' Palace, and Il Redentore on the Giudecca. The former not only has perfection of design, but also perfection of position. Standing in the Piazzetta looking out over the basin of St. Mark's, one realizes that without Palladio's

Henry James, whose infatuation with Venice is evident in the pages of his evocative Italian Hours, *called the Church of San Giorgio Maggiore (below) "a success beyond all reason." In part, James was lauding Andrea Palladio, the facile Paduan who designed the island church's classical façade; in part, he was commending the building's location, directly across St. Mark's basin from the Doges' Palace. In a sense, the great church — which rises from the very tip of the island of San Giorgio — serves both to frame the basin and to close and complete the southern vista of the Piazzetta.*

domed neoclassical church and tall, slender campanile, there would be no view at all, only an empty stretch of water. Although situated in the lagoon, San Giorgio somehow completes the Doges' Palace and the whole basin of St. Mark's. The same is true of the less successful Il Redentore, for without it the Giudecca would have practically no skyline at all.

Palladio's greatest work, however, was done on terra firma. It was one of those rare coincidences — the right patrons, the right artist, the right times. A patrician class with money, leisure, and taste, anxious to establish landed estates, and an architect of consummate mastery, born, as it were, to fulfill its needs. The results: Villa della Malcontenta, with its huge temple portico, built for the Foscari family on the Brenta Canal; La Rotunda, built for the Valmaranas outside Vicenza and subsequently reproduced many times in England; and Andrea Palladio's incomparable Villa Barbaro at Maser.

Writing of his plans for the Villa Barbaro, Palladio asserted that "the beauty will spring from the relationship of the whole to the parts, of the parts to each other, and of the parts to the whole." And indeed the first impression the visitor to Maser has is one of a perfectly ordered harmony. Porticoes, rooms, staircases, windows, nymphaea, gardens, forests, orchards, fountains, parks — all are arranged so as to complement and balance one another. To live in Villa Barbaro was to live in a perfectly ordered world of harmony, light, and beauty. Berenson observed that this gracious standard of living gave the tone to the whole of sixteenth and seventeenth-century Europe, adding that "because there was a class that could live that way, the humblest of today live more comfortably than great lords of eight hundred, even four hundred, years ago." It was an enormous tribute to Palladio that centuries after his death architects in Great Britain and the American South, anxious to please wealthy patrons, could do no better than imitate his Venetian villas.

While Andrea Palladio was building monuments to the wealth and prestige of Venice's greatest patrician families, and while Paolo Veronese was glorifying Venice on the ceiling of the Doges' Palace, the Most Serene Republic itself began to suffer its first serious losses in the East, the prelude to its long, drawn-out decline. In 1537, she had fought a brief naval war with the Turks, one that ended in a military stalemate and ultimately in political surrender for the Venetians. The ensuing negotiations proved disastrous, for the Venetian envoy was betrayed by a confidant of the Council of Ten. Horrified by the betrayal, the Ten formed a Council of Three to deal with matters of security, and that inner council gradually assumed the preponderant power in the republic.

Thirty-three years after the formation of the Council of Three, war with the Turks broke out again, this time with even more disastrous consequences for Venice. In 1570, the Turkish sultan laid siege to Nicosia, capital of Cyprus. The Venetians halfheartedly dispatched a fleet commanded by Nicolo Dandolo, a descendant of the blind doge who had led the Fourth Crusade, and after a brief clash during which neither he nor his men displayed anything resembling the bravery of their ancestors, Dandolo surrendered. In the slaughter that followed he was decapitated, and his head was hurled over the walls of the Venetian fortress

The carefree mood characteristic of Veronese's domestic scenes is appropriately absent from the complex historical panorama at left, which recreates the stunning Venetian victory over the Turkish fleet at Lepanto in 1571. Decisive as that defeat was – the Turks lost 25,000 men and the bulk of their navy – it did not long deter Ottoman corsairs from attacking Venetian shipping in the Levant. Indeed, Venice found herself involved in naval clashes with the Turks throughout the sixteenth century. The bas-relief at right, which adorns a seventeenth-century Venetian church, recalls one such engagement in the ongoing contest.

at Famagusta, which was subsequently brought under siege. The commander of the fortress, Marcantonio Bragadin, put up a long and brave defense, but in August 1571 he was finally forced to surrender. The Turks offered him safe conduct, then went back on their word. They arrested him, tortured him, chained him to a post in the main square of Famagusta, and whipped him to death. Later his skin, stuffed with straw, was taken to Constantinople and displayed in the Turkish arsenal. This outrage was not without beneficial results, however, for it rekindled Venetian fighting spirit, forced Venice into alliance with her traditional enemies – Spain, Genoa, and the papacy – and eventually brought the once-invincible Ottoman Turks to their knees.

In late September 1571, a combined fleet of two hundred galleys, twenty transports, fifty light craft, and six huge galleasses, manned by 50,000 sailors and 30,000 soldiers, set sail for the Gulf of Corinth to confront the infidel.

The clash proved to be one of the greatest naval battles in history. The sultan's fleet of three hundred vessels, including two hundred galleys, lay in wait off Lepanto. Galley rammed galley, and in the midst of the battle the two flagships even rammed each other. The air was rent with the cries of chained slaves crushed in their oar banks, the snapping of oars and masts, the booming of countless cannon. The clangor and the carnage, which lasted all day, is depicted in a painting by Paolo Veronese. It shows the sea jammed with colliding warships and strewn with oars, masts, pennants, and corpses – the detritus of a battle that took 8,000 Christian lives and left 16,000 wounded. The Turks, for their part, had lost 25,000 men and practically their entire fleet.

After the battle of Lepanto, a certain complacency set in among the allies. Having thrashed the infidels, they felt that they could return to business as usual. Soon they were quarreling among themselves – Spain, Genoa, and the papacy turning once more against Venice – and the Turkish corsairs were again attacking Christian fleets. The great victory had not been followed up, and as a result Venice found herself no better off vis-à-vis the Turks than before, despite her expenditure of lives and money. Cyprus was still in Turkish hands; the republic's other eastern possessions, especially Crete, were as vulnerable as ever; and Venetian merchants were still denied access to many of the Eastern markets they had once monopolized. By the end of the sixteenth century, the Most Serene Republic's treasury was seriously depleted, many patrician families were bankrupt, and the warehouses on the Rialto and the Giudecca that had once bulged with Oriental silks, brocades, spices, and perfumes were as depleted as the treasury.

To add to her misfortunes, Venice fell under papal interdiction in 1606. Throughout the sixteenth century, the Most Serene Republic had remained more independent from the papacy than the other states of the Italian peninsula, but relations had always been cordial. Then, in the first decade of the seventeenth century, she openly defied the newly elected pope, Paul V. The issue was simple and clear-cut: the Venetians had always insisted that the patriarch of Venice and the city's other high church officials be Venetian-born, and they had also insisted that the doge, and only the doge,

This remarkably comprehensive overview of Venice and its watery environs, the work of Ignazio Danti, a noted sixteenth-century cartographer, shows the lagoon city bisected by the sweeping curve of the Grand Canal. North of the lagoon, the foothills of the Italian Alps loom above terra firma, Venice's holdings on the mainland. The island of San Giorgio Maggiore and the long crescent of the Giudecca lie south of the city, sheltered from the unpredictable Adriatic by the Lido littoral.

could appoint the patriarch. Upon assuming office, Paul V contested this practice and ordered the newly appointed patriarch to Rome to be interviewed and confirmed. The republic summarily refused, and the pope became enraged.

Paul V was also irritated at the Venetians because he considered them too lenient on those who had committed offenses against the church. Time and again the Venetians refused to turn wayward priests and supposed heretics over to papal inquisitors, preferring instead to have them tried before the Council of Ten, who punished felonious clerics by imprisoning them in a cage hung from a window of the Campanile. There was, in addition, the case of British Ambassador Henry Wolton, who was suspected of smuggling secret Protestant books into the city — and of actually daring to hold Anglican services in the British embassy in Venice. The Venetians turned a deaf ear to all the pope's complaints, just as they had done for centuries.

Egged on by the Spanish, who were exasperated that Venice and only Venice remained independent of their control in Italy, Paul V declared Venice excommunicate in April 1606 and expelled the Venetian ambassador to the holy see. Venice reacted by reaffirming the doge's exclusive prerogative to appoint the patriarch of Venice and declaring, through the Serenissima Signoria, that she considered Pope Paul's excommunication to be totally invalid.

All this would not have been very serious for Venice if it had not been for the fact that many northern merchants, upon receiving word of the interdict, cancelled shipments to and from the Serene Republic. Venice was now trading upon her accumulated prestige, acting as if she were still the Olympian, indomitable, utterly autonomous Serenissima. The truth was that although she would emerge from the struggle relatively unscarred, she could ill afford to take such gambles. For by the time of the Great Interdict, she had become more isolated than ever from the church and the other Italian states. Spain was still her sworn enemy in the West, her monetary reserves were the lowest in centuries, many of her aristocrats were beggared, her warehouses were half empty, and her trade with the East was thwarted at every crossroad and bazaar by the Ottoman Turks. No one in Venice would admit it, but La Serenissima, though outwardly magnificent, had passed her peak and was entering a long decline.

Murano
S. Iacomo
S. Nicolo
Mazorbo
Burano
S. Secondo
S. Angelo
S. Michiel
S. Christofano
Lazaretto nouo
Arsenale
Vergini
S. Marco
S. Giorgio maggiore
S. Lazaro
S. Seruolo
Lazaretto vecchio
S. Clemente
S. Spirito
Giudeca
Malamocho

V

The Age of the Baroque

As the Venetian ship of state sailed into the seventeenth century – cannons loaded, banners flying, as proud and seemingly triumphant as ever – three enemies lay waiting in her path: the papacy, Spain, and the Ottoman Turks. All three were sighted by the officers in charge, but they failed to detect a fourth enemy, one that lurked like a dormant cancer among the officers themselves. That foe was a new softness of resolve, a growing reluctance to fight that would prove the most formidable threat of all.

The sea upon which Venice sailed – Italy in the seventeenth century – has been called the Age of the Baroque. The term "baroque," first used to describe certain tendencies in the arts, later became associated with such specific social and political conditions as absolute monarchy, aristocratic privilege, church censorship, and the regimentation and bureaucratization of daily life – all of which were present in seventeenth-century Italy. During the Age of the Baroque, Europe's absolute monarchs – in league with the Spanish viceroys in Naples and Milan, and the Spanish puppet in Florence – managed to eliminate all rivals, suppress all political activity that challenged their authority, and thus reign without significant opposition. The Spanish viceroy of Naples ruled southern Italy as representative of the king of Spain, and virtually all state power was centered in his hands. The pope, meanwhile, ruled the Papal States as an absolute monarch. All opposition to his temporal authority was discouraged by the presence of a Spanish regiment whose dual role was to protect the pope from his potential enemies and assure his obedience to the will of Spain. To the north, the Medici reigned supreme in an enlarged Tuscany, where opposition to *their* rule was thwarted by a Spanish garrison that was stationed in Fort Belvedere, not far from Pitti Palace. In Milan, a Spanish viceroy with headquarters in the Castello Sforzesco ruled the duchy as a virtual dictator.

As the bureaucratic organization of these small but powerful states tightened, Italy became enmeshed in a web of strict administrative controls: economic activities were rigidly regulated, and the laissez-faire economy of the Renaissance gradually disappeared. Price controls were established, a complicated system of commercial licensing was instituted, and heavy taxes were imposed upon the population. Behind these controls stood the omnipresent Spanish garrisons, ready to enforce them if necessary.

Equally rigid and oppressive was the Counter-Reform church, which cracked down on the peninsula's intellectual and artistic life through the Index and the Inquisition, establishing canons of literary and artistic taste. Behind *these* regulations also stood the Spanish garrisons, ready to enforce the church's dictates. This new regimentation of thought was exemplified by the Society of Jesus, which had been founded in 1540 by the Spanish nobleman Ignatius Loyola to combat Protestantism and reform the intellectual and moral life of the church. The Jesuit order was organized like an army, and its soldiers of Jesus were to be found in every school, university, library, courtroom, church, and ducal palace in Italy. Rigidly disciplined, the Jesuits attracted outstanding men to their ranks and soon came to dominate Italian intellectual life, employing a brand of eloquence that was as flamboyantly baroque as the churches in which it was declaimed.

Socially the period was one of progressive aristocratization. Society became rigidly stratified into two classes: the Grandi Signori, titled noblemen who became all-powerful and decidedly overprivileged; and the vast, often poverty-stricken mob who were literally powerless. It was the opinion of Benedetto Croce, the Neapolitan philosopher, that the centuries of Spanish domination permanently warped the Italian national character — and there is little question that during the sixteenth, seventeenth, and early eighteenth centuries, Italians of both classes lost their moral integrity.

Throughout the seventeenth century, the Venetian ship of state displayed considerable ingenuity in avoiding the twin reefs of Spain and the papacy. In her struggle to remain independent of the pope and the Inquisition and in defiance of the Great Interdict of 1606, the Serenissima Signoria employed the brilliant mind of Fra Paolo Sarpi, a Servite brother and theologian who had helped Galileo construct the first telescope. Sarpi's cleverly reasoned justifications for Venice's continued intractability confounded even the Jesuits, who eventually packed their black bags and returned to Rome. Meanwhile, Venetian parish priests and bishops continued to hold church services and administer the sacraments as if the Great Interdict had never existed.

After much wrangling — during which Fra Sarpi was pitted directly against the pope himself, much to the delectation of the Protestants — the ban was lifted without Venice's having to sacrifice one shred of her autonomy. When the affair was over, Sarpi was summoned to Rome to explain his position. He wisely refused to go, only to be waylaid by papal bravos on a narrow bridge near the Campo di Santa Fosca in October of 1607 and stabbed three times. He survived to eventually take his place among the great heroes of the Venetian Republic.

Ten years after the papal threat was disposed of, the menacing hulk of Spain loomed on the Venetian horizon. Over the years, La Serenissima had helped many mainland princes in their struggles to remain free of Spanish domination. This subversive posture, coupled with the humiliating fact that Venice had succeeded in remaining outside the Spanish orbit entirely, so irritated the Spanish that they resolved to put an end to La Serenissima once and for all by means of a bold coup d'etat. The so-called Spanish Plot was hatched by the viceroy of Naples, the governor of Milan, and the marquis of Bedmar, Spanish ambassador to Venice. Their plan was to seize the Lido with a fleet from Naples; land a Spanish army on the Piazzetta; destroy the Doges' Palace, the Arsenale, and the mint; and capture the doge and the members of the Great Council. The coup was to take place on Ascension Day, when the doge and his cabinets would be afloat on the lagoon in the defenseless Bucentaur.

All was in readiness — and the Spanish were exulting in advance over having finally bent La Serenissima to their rule — when the plot was discovered. A Venetian senator named Bragadin, a friend of the marquis of Bedmar and a coconspirator, left a compromising note in the Church of I Frari, where it was found by a suspicious friar and turned over to the Council of Ten. The next day the Venetians were shocked to find a string of corpses hanging in the Piazzetta between the columns of St. Mark and St. Theodore. The Ten had

The Bridge of Sighs (left) was constructed in the late sixteenth century to connect the Doges' Palace with a squat and forbidding prison on the opposite bank of the Rio di Palazzo. Political prisoners sentenced by the all-powerful Council of Ten were led across the short marble span to the pozzi, *the dank, canal-level cells of the prison — and the plaintive cries they uttered in passing gave the bridge its name. Over the centuries, the infamous* pozzi *held doges and generals as well as renegades and rogues. One who narrowly escaped such a fate was Francesco Morosini, the resourceful admiral who held the Venetian garrison on Crete through some thirty-odd Turkish assaults before surrendering. When Morosini returned to Venice, the irate Ten stripped him of his command. Reinstated fifteen years later, Morosini affixed his personal pennant (right) to a warship's prow and set sail for the East. This time, his valor was rewarded with a dogeship.*

not wasted any time, and before they were through, more than three hundred conspirators were either hanged, strangled, or drowned.

In the decades following the bloody resolution of the Spanish Plot, the Most Serene Republic gradually turned into a police state. The Council of Three acquired ever-increasing power — sufficient, in time, to challenge the Council of Ten, of which they were members. The Three sent their spies out into every corner of the city, and no citizen could be sure he was not being listened to or watched by an informer. If a Venetian was accused of a treasonable act, or even a treasonable intention, justice was swift. The accused was arraigned in the Sala della Bussola in the Doges' Palace, a room connected by two camouflaged doors to the Hall of the Ten and the Hall of the Three. The Sala della Bussola was also connected by corridors and stairways to the two prisons, the *piombi* and the *pozzi.* If convicted, a prisoner faced a short walk to confinement: either up a narrow stairway to the hot, suffocating *piombi* under the roof, or down another stairway and over the Bridge of Sighs to the cold, dark, often flooded *pozzi* at canal level. Venetians of the period took to saying, "The Ten send you to the torture chambers; the Three to your grave."

With the pope and Spain at bay, the Most Serene Republic turned its attention to its third enemy: the Ottoman Turks, who began threatening Crete in April 1645. That war dragged on for twenty-four years. At the time it began, the Venetian treasury was already so depleted that the state had to insist that every citizen hand in three-quarters of his gold and silver plate to help pay for the war. And when this proved insufficient,

Working within exacting financial, structural, and aesthetic guidelines dictated by the city fathers, Baldassare Longhena created the most brilliant architectural jewel in the Venetian diadem — the soaring baroque Church of Santa Maria della Salute (right). Built as a votive church to commemorate the end of the devastating plague of 1629, La Salute lifts its gleaming drum of white Istrian stone high above the surrounding tiled rooftops, its silhouette dominating the southern terminus of the Grand Canal. The building's open design (left) was without precedent in Venetian architecture, and as a result the lambent nave of La Salute is without peer in a city filled with churches.

the state took to financing the conflict by offering important government posts and patents of nobility to the highest bidders. Under the new dispensation, if a commoner could prove that he was a legitimate offspring of a man who was not a manual laborer, and if he had the necessary funds, he could enter the hitherto sacrosanct ranks of the patricians. The prospect was so enticing that many prosperous merchants impoverished themselves for the privilege of sitting in the Great Council and inscribing their children's names in the Golden Book.

But the gold and silver plate of the people and the life savings of the parvenu nobles were not enough to finance the war with the Turks. More even than money, the Venetians needed nerve, the willingness to fight as hard to defend their overseas possessions as they had to conquer them. This is not to say that there were not flashes of the old bravery. In 1654, for example, forty Venetian galleys took on a hundred Turkish galleys in the Dardanelles and burned eighty-five of them. And Admiral Francesco Morosini, during the final siege of the Cretan capital, repelled no fewer than seventeen sorties and thirty-two assaults. But throughout the long war, the Venetians displayed little of the old resolve to fight, and time and again the republic had to rely on reinforcements from such hastily recruited "allies" as the papacy, Naples, and Tuscany. Finally, on September 27, 1669, Francesco Morosini and the remnants of his garrison surrendered. The cost to the republic had been enormous: 30,000 Venetians were dead, Crete was lost, untold sums of money had gone down the drain — and perhaps worst of all, Venice stood humiliated before the world.

When he returned home with his surviving forces, Francesco Morosini was promptly relieved of his command by the Ten. Fifteen years later, however, the sixty-six-year-old admiral, a member of one of Venice's greatest ducal families, was pardoned and reappointed commander in chief. In a brilliant subsequent campaign, during which the Venetians showed occasional sparks of the old fire, Morosini reconquered parts of the Peloponnesus and all of Athens.

Morosini was elected doge in 1688 and served for five years before sailing eastward to fight the Turks again. Like Enrico Dandolo, who had made a nearly identical journey five centuries before, Morosini never returned. By the end of 1715, the Peloponnesus was again in Turkish hands, and by 1718, Venice's overseas empire had shrunk to include only the Ionian islands, Istria, and the coast of Dalmatia.

From this point on, the Venetian aristocrats rapidly lost their taste for adventure and combat, preferring the calm and comfort of their villas on terra firma to the Spartan life of galley and garrison. Venice grew reluctant to fight even defensive wars; attacks on overseas possessions elicited notes of protest, but no counterattacks. It is an interesting commentary on the Venetian psychology at the time that even after the republic lost Cyprus and Crete, their flags were still flown each holiday from the great masts in front of St. Mark's. By the eighteenth century, appearance counted more than reality to the Venetians.

It would be unfair, however, to give the impression that Venice knew only loss and progressive enfeeblement during these years. She reacted to many crises with her usual strength and determination; and her

painters, architects, and composers continued to enrich the city with works of originality and great beauty. One of the gravest crises came to a head during the first decade of the seventeenth century. For years the water magistrates, those officials of the republic concerned with problems of the lagoon, had been noting with increasing alarm that the lagoon was slowly but inexorably silting up. If the process were allowed to continue, Venice's impregnable position would be jeopardized and her channels and harbors would become unfit for shipping. The water magistrates were invested with absolute authority in matters relating to the equilibrium between land and sea in the lagoon, and it was up to them to decide what to do about the silting. For decades the matter was debated, but when the magistrates made their decision to deviate the three rivers that were causing the silting, they stuck to it — and thereby saved Venice from sure extinction.

During the early 1600's, the republic was still capable of completing Herculean architectural projects as well, and it produced another architect of genius, a fitting successor to Palladio, to undertake them. The architect was Baldassare Longhena, and it is to him that credit must go for the completion of the urban masterwork that is Venice. To substantiate this statement, we need only contemplate what Venice would look like without Longhena's buildings.

Venice without the Church of Santa Maria della Salute, the Procuratie Nuove, the monastery of San Giorgio, Ca' Rezzonico, and the Palazzo Pesaro would not be the Venice we know today. La Salute, for example, literally creates the entrance to the Grand Canal, giving it grandeur and authority. Its huge dome,

Plague was a frequent visitor to European ports during the late Middle Ages, the dreaded result of a vastly expanded trade with the Orient. The full fury of the Black Death broke over Venice in 1576, leaving 40,000 corpses in its wake. Fifty-three years later, a second major epidemic carried off nearly one-quarter of the republic's population. In their desperation, the Venetians raised La Salute — an ex-voto offering to Our Lady of Health and Salvation — in hopes that their city would be spared further devastation. Dominating the view from the main doorway of La Salute is a statue group (below) dedicated to the city's miraculous deliverance. It includes a personification of the plague as an old hag (lower right) being driven from Venice by the Virgin Mary.

when seen from the lagoon, balances perfectly the cupola and the Campanile of St. Mark's. The immense Procuratie Nuove, which replaced dozens of small hotels and shops, completes Piazza San Marco, forming its southern boundary. The monastery of San Giorgio provides a much needed complement to Palladio's church, and the grandeur of Ca' Rezzonico and the Palazzo Pesaro, the last great palaces built along the Grand Canal, give the canal an added monumentality. It was Longhena, then, who put the icing on the cake; it was his finishing touches that perfected the Venice we know and love today.

Baldassare Longhena, who was born in 1604, sixteen years after Veronese's death, was a short, intense man who dressed only in black and was utterly obsessed with architecture. His contemporaries inform us that whenever he met a friend he would immediately ask him for an opinion of his current work-in-progress, and at cafes and dinner parties he would often break off a conversation to sketch a design in his notebook. Longhena's greatest creation is the huge, octagonal Church of Santa Maria della Salute, popularly known as La Salute and unquestionably the supreme masterpiece of Venetian baroque architecture.

The church was commissioned in 1630 by the Venetian Senate as an offering to Our Lady of Health, in the hopes that she would intervene to save Venice from the plague. A plague had struck the city in 1576, taking 40,000 lives, including Titian's, and in 1629 another had struck, carrying off a quarter of the population. In the midst of this horror, the Senate announced a competition for the construction of an ex-voto church. A committee of senators chose the site, a spot near the

La Salute had been abuilding for thirty years when Baldassare Longhena tackled his second major assignment along the Grand Canal, the creation of a truly lavish and imposing private residence. From its massive, rusticated façade to its dazzling, translucent chandeliers (right), Ca' Rezzonico embodied the finest in design and decoration. For the nouveau riche Rezzonico family, money was no object, and they unhesitatingly engaged Tiepolo and Guardi to decorate the walls and ceilings of their palazzo's main reception rooms.

customhouse at the entrance to the Grand Canal, ordered all the buildings in the area demolished, and had the corps of engineers drive no fewer than 1,156,627 wooden piles down into the hard clay to provide a solid foundation.

Precise guidelines were established for the construction. The church was to be designed so that the entire interior could be understood visually as soon as one entered. There was to be an equal distribution of bright light throughout the space, and the high altar was to dominate the view from the main door, the other altars coming into view only as the visitor approached the high altar. The architect was further required to erect a building that would harmonize with the site and make a brilliant impression, a *bellissima figura,* without costing too much. Eleven architects presented designs to these specifications, and Longhena won. Construction, which would last fifty-seven years, began immediately.

La Salute is an extraordinarily powerful work of art. The white marble octagonal structure with its huge main dome, two campaniles, and smaller cupola dominates the Venetian skyline, looming even larger than St. Mark's. Indeed, Longhena fulfilled the Senate's intentions to the letter. As one enters the church, one's attention is immediately riveted upon the grandiose main altar, and yet because of the almost circular construction one is aware also of the entire extent of the church. The gray stone and whitewashed plaster of the walls give the interior a quiet, cool appearance, but there is always a great abundance of light, even on overcast days. Longhena himself observed of La Salute that "the mystery contained in its dedication to the Blessed Virgin made me think with what little talent God has given me, of building it in a circular form, that is to say in the shape of a crown to be dedicated to the Virgin." If one bears this statement in mind when visiting the church or observing it from outside, one senses how brilliantly Longhena realized his intention. The church *is* a crown, crowning both the Virgin and Venice.

Longhena's other baroque masterpieces, Ca' Rezzonico and the Palazzo Pesaro, are perhaps the most imposing palaces on the Grand Canal because of their enormous size and extravagant decoration. Both have massive, rusticated bases and extremely elaborate façades broken up by a profusion of columns, windows, balconies, and loggias. Baldassare Longhena did not live to complete Ca' Rezzonico, which he began for another patron and which the Rezzonico family purchased in an unfinished state after buying their way into the Venetian aristocracy for the colossal sum of 160,000 ducats (roughly $15,000,000 today).

Baldassare Longhena brought the baroque style to Venice and adapted it brilliantly to Venetian needs. The impact of his style was so profound that virtually all the city's painters and architects turned to the baroque, thus giving Venice a third distinct style, a kind of overlay on top of the Gothic and Renaissance.

The baroque style originated in Rome as a response to the disasters that overwhelmed Renaissance Italy in the sixteenth century. During that period, writers and artists had broken with the God-centered outlook of the medieval period to idealize the powers and aspirations of mortal men. This new faith had borne fruit during a century of unparalleled achievement in virtually every field of human endeavor; unhappily, it had also cre-

The elevation at left shows the surpassingly elegant residence that Longhena designed in the 1660's as it looked after Giorgio Massari added another story in the eighteenth century. At the time that Ca' Rezzonico was begun, Venice was enjoying a period of unparalleled commercial prosperity and concomitant personal affluence. The contemporary drawing at right reveals the degree to which even such mundane objects as gondolas were embellished during this freespending era.

ated a climate in which ruthless egotism flourished unchecked. As a result, the late Renaissance was also witness to the spectacle of a selfish drive for power that often involved the commission of serious crimes.

Thus while Renaissance humanism in Italy helped produce a magnificent civilization in Rome, Florence, and Venice, it simultaneously created a climate of rivalry and disunity that caused the entire country, with the sole exception of Venice, to fall under the domination of a tyrannical foreign power. Italy's prosperity was undermined, and her international prestige was deflated. As a result, her artists and writers began to lose the exalted faith in man that they had inherited from the previous century. They grew increasingly pessimistic about man's ability to control his own destiny, to shape the world in accordance with his desires. And yet they could not go back to a wholly God-centered outlook; they could no longer accept a world in which man was but an instrument of the divine will.

Having lost their faith in both God and man, the artists and writers of the late sixteenth and early seventeenth centuries entered a period of profound spiritual crisis – and out of this crisis came a new style and a new outlook: the baroque. This style, with its florid, theatrical effects, was a quintessentially Italian response to acute spiritual suffering. It was a response to a diminution of faith in God and man, as well as a response to the suffocating oppression of the Spanish regime and the Catholic church. Deprived of deep convictions and humiliated by the presence of a tyrannical foreign power, prideful Italian painters, sculptors, architects, and writers attempted to compensate by making a concerted effort to impress, to astonish – to make, in spite of everything, a *bellissima figura.* Hence the histrionic flourish and bravura of so much baroque art, the overemphasis on inconsequential details, the polychromatic richness of interiors, the importance attached to façade.

Although Venice was spared much of the suffering that Naples, Rome, and Florence endured, the baroque style and outlook were nevertheless eminently suited to fulfill her deepest psychological needs in the late seventeenth century. La Serenissima had lost Cyprus and Crete by that time, and she was well on her way to losing the Peloponnesus. She had lost her monopoly on Oriental trade; the Atlantic had replaced the Mediterranean as the primary avenue of Western European commerce; there was no longer full employment in the Arsenale; and many patrician families were bankrupt. In such uncertain times, it must have been a great consolation to the Venetians, now afflicted with self-doubt, to see the gigantic form of La Salute rising on the Grand Canal.

Critics generally agree that architecture fared much better than painting during the baroque age in Venice, for during the seventeenth century Venetian artists did little more than imitate – badly – the great masters of the past, particularly Giorgione, Titian, and Veronese. It was not until Giovanni Battista Tiepolo began painting in the early eighteenth century that Venetian art received fresh inspiration from a first-rate talent.

To Tiepolo belongs the distinction of being the last great Venetian artist. A true genius, he blossomed young and he painted rapidly and without effort. His output was enormous, even greater than Titian's, and although he obviously borrowed much from Veronese, he was a highly original artist with a style unmistak-

ably his own. Théophile Gautier once called Tiepolo "the great master of decadence," but Berenson claimed that he was "not so much the last of the old masters, but the first of the new." Perhaps he was both — decadent because of his escapist subject matter; "first of the new" because of his almost impressionistic style. Whichever way one looks at Tiepolo, one thing is certain: the Most Serene Republic's eighteenth-century decline produced not a pall but a sunburst — and much of that blaze was generated by Tiepolo.

The son of a well-to-do merchant, "Giambattista" Tiepolo was born in Venice in 1696, 108 years after the death of his spiritual father, Paolo Veronese. His remarkable talent was recognized at an early age, and he was sent to the studio of the history painter Gregorio Lazzarini for a grounding in technique. At nineteen, while he was still with Lazzarini, Tiepolo completed his first major work, *The Sacrifice of Isaac,* for the Church of Santa Maria dei Derelitti. Tiepolo's extraordinary facility as a decorator soon brought him international fame and commissions from the crowned heads of Europe. Among the most important of these were the decoration of the Palazzo Labia and Ca' Rezzonico in Venice, the Villa Pisani at Stra, and imperial residences in Würzburg and Madrid.

Tiepolo was preeminently a painter of glorious, sunlit skies — skies full of fluffy, white clouds, floating gods and goddesses, and golden chariots soaring into the blue. So delightful are his vast ceiling decorations that we get the impression he was only really at home in the clouds, away from the vulgarities of earthbound man. When he does come down to earth and paints figures with their feet on the ground, he is usually unconvincing; these lovely, gossamer people are so insubstantial that they belong only in the sky. More than any other Venetian artist, Tiepolo glories in light. His is the sort of light one finds on the Lido, a beach light that turns colors chalky, a light under which no other tones can exist but pastels. All Tiepolo's winged sky creatures seem to float toward the light, and the faces of his gods and heroes are bleached by it.

While Tiepolo was glorifying patricians, saints, princes, and kings in his luminous sky frescoes, his near contemporary Antonio Canale, known as Canaletto, was busy painting the city of Venice. Although Tiepolo and Canaletto were both enamored with light, the two artists were otherwise radically different. Tiepolo's art is wholly imaginative, whereas Canaletto's work is of an almost photographic realism. It is as if the two artists looked in diametrically opposite directions, for in all Tiepolo's vast opus there is hardly a drop of water, while Canaletto is invariably most at home along the waterways of his beloved Venice. Canaletto was not a great artist — his powers of imagination were too slight — but he was an extremely competent and accurate one. Moreover, he performed an invaluable service for posterity, for his views of Venice provide a unique and extraordinary portrait of La Serenissima at the time of her fading glory.

Canaletto's conception of Venice was essentially a positive one. The artist appears to have taken a genuine delight in the calm, unhurried depiction of what he saw. There is a painstaking precision to his work, a care for topographical accuracy that borders on what Ruskin called "servile and mindless imitation." His paintings are wonderfully detailed, and one marvels at

The wealth of the Labia family was prodigious, and their extravagance prodigal. They squandered staggering sums on entertainment, fêting hundreds of guests at a time in any of their dozens of opulent residences in Venice and on the mainland. The family's principal residence, on the Canale di Cannaregio, contains one of the most beautiful salons in the entire city. Its walls are entirely covered with frescoes by Giovanni Battista Tiepolo, whose bright, clear palette led some to call him the foremost painter in Italy, others to label him the greatest of all eighteenth-century painters. The fresco cycle that Tiepolo executed for the Labias, delineating the tragic tale of Antony and Cleopatra, includes a panel known as The Embarkation *(left). Meticulous as well as talented, Tiepolo produced scores of preliminary sketches for the cycle, among them the busy figure study at right.*

his ability to include so much minutiae in such relatively small canvases. At his worst, Canaletto is merely photographic; at best, he conveys a subdued poetry, an obvious love for what he is painting that can be very appealing.

An exhibition of Canaletto's work in 1725 brought him international recognition, and Europeans – especially Englishmen – began buying his paintings as souvenirs of Venice. He soon found that he could not turn canvases out fast enough. He hiked his prices, and his paintings sold even more briskly. Before long it became extremely difficult to purchase a Canaletto, and wealthy Englishmen outbid one another for his works, paying him twice what he asked. In 1730, the British consul in Venice, Joseph Smith, became a middleman for the artist, selling his paintings on commission and making considerable sums of money in the process. In 1746, Canaletto went to England, where he painted, with varying degrees of success, an extensive series of English views. Because his subject matter – both early and late – appealed much more to the British than to his own countrymen, there are scores of Canalettos in England, but only a half dozen in Venice itself.

Neither Canaletto nor Tiepolo enjoyed extraordinary fame or popularity in their native city. Tiepolo's greatest patrons and admirers were the prince of Würzburg and the king of Spain, and Canaletto was the darling of the English. The truth was that during the seventeenth and eighteenth centuries, Venice was much more a city of music than a city of painting. The Venetians, in their decline, turned to music with an appetite unmatched by any people in history. Music offered consolations on a scale that painters were unable to equal, and as these consolations became more and more vital to the Venetian psyche, the city became a perpetual music festival. Concerts were held every night of the week, and it was not uncommon for listeners to faint from rapture during particularly moving works.

Nietzche has claimed that nostalgia is a fundamental stimulus to musical composition, that a culture produces its deepest and most intense musical expression not during its ascendance but during its decline, when its memories are long and poignant. No civilization illustrates this contention better than Venice, for as La Serenissima's wealth and power waned, Venetia (or the Veneto, as it was now known) gave birth to at least four first-rate composers – Arcangelo Corelli, Tommaso Albinoni, Antonio Vivaldi, and Benedetto Marcello – and dozens of excellent minor ones. Their music was the republic's last great gift to the world.

By the time these composers appeared on the scene, Venice already possessed the finest musical tradition in Europe. Music had been particularly congenial in Venice, where motets, cantatas, passions, and oratorios had been a part of all ceremonies and pageants. Her composers were always in the avant-garde, and Giovanni Gabrieli, who was director of music at St. Mark's in the early 1600's, was the foremost Italian composer of his day. His immensely self-assured, triumphant polyphonic works for multiple choruses, brass choirs, and orchestras – often performed stereophonically in St. Mark's with choruses and orchestras spaced throughout the basilica – were renowned from Paris to Rome. Moreover, they set the stage for his immediate successor, Monteverdi, who is best known for having laid the foundation for grand opera. In 1607, his seminal

opera *Orpheus* was produced in Florence, and after he moved to Venice he introduced opera to the Venetians, who embraced the new art form with enormous enthusiasm. Opera not only appealed to the Venetians' musical sense, but also to their love of pageantry and visual splendor. In 1643, the first permanent opera house in the Western world was opened in Venice. By then Monteverdi and his followers had produced some thirty operas, several of which are still performed today. Such was the success of opera in Venice that by the end of the century there were no less than fifteen opera houses in the city.

After Monteverdi's development of opera came the creation of the modern orchestral concerto by Arcangelo Corelli. The word *concerto,* which means "playing together," had previously been used to describe religious works for organ and voices; Corelli was the first composer to create works in which a group of solo instruments were pitted against a large orchestral background, and he labeled these compositions "concerti." The new form had far-ranging influence, stimulating Handel to write his concerti grossi and Albinoni, Marcello, and Vivaldi to produce their variations.

Orchestral music in eighteenth-century Venice was generally performed in patrician palaces and in the city's four *ospedali,* or "asylums" for foundling girls: the Mendicanti, the Pietà, the Incurabili, and the Ospedaletto. The inmates of these institutions were raised and educated at the state's expense, and each asylum maintained a music conservatory and an orchestra. The girls were said to play all instruments and to sing "like angels," and many of them had fanatical followings.

Audiences at these performances were extremely disciplined and attentive, and the girls captivated and enchanted their listeners. After a performance the musicians would often mingle with the audience, and some girls reportedly found husbands among the listeners. Rousseau once remarked that the music of the orphan girls of Venice was the most moving he had ever heard, and Goethe agreed, noting that he had never heard anything so rapturous as the singing of the Mendicanti.

Antonio Vivaldi, Venice's greatest composer, was in charge of music at the Conservatorio dell'Ospedale della Pietà. A red-bearded priest and virtuoso violinist, he was gifted with inexhaustible creative energy. Besides directing the conservatory and playing and teaching the violin, he wrote more than four hundred concerti, fifty-three sonatas, forty church pieces, and forty operas. Legend has it that while celebrating mass, he would suddenly be struck by inspiration, leave the altar, and race to the sacristy to jot the idea down.

Vivaldi's music has both a wildly ecstatic quality and a serene, often slightly melancholy repose that is typically Venetian. His allegros are among the most joyful in all of Western music, glittering tone pageants that are as bright and clear and happy as the lagoon on a sunny morning. There is a smooth, easy, almost liquid fluency to his work that denotes a consummate mastery of craft. Every allegro is as triumphant an affirmation of faith as St. Mark's, the Doges' Palace, or La Salute. But there is a melancholy side to Venice also, one that Vivaldi expressed with equal mastery.

Vivaldi is best known to concert audiences today for his two sets of concerti grossi, *L'Estro armonico,* which contains twelve pieces, and *Il Cimento dell'Armonia e*

Seventeenth-century Venice's most enduring cultural monument may well prove to be musical rather than architectural, for during that period the republic produced three widely influential composers and two fresh musical forms: Claudio Monteverdi introduced opera to an enchanted and enthusiastic city, Arcangelo Corelli popularized the modern orchestral concerto, and Antonio Vivaldi later created more than four hundred such concerti. The sculptors who decorated La Salute acknowledged their fellow artists by adding the cherubim at left, each of whom is playing a different musical instrument.

Overleaf:

No Venetian artist celebrated the untarnished glories of Venice at her imperial apogee more fully or more fervently than Antonio Canale, known to the foreigners who avidly collected his serene, highly colored works as Canaletto. Indeed, views such as this one of the Piazza San Marco were so popular abroad that few of them remain in Venice.

dell'Invenzione, which includes the group of concerti known as "The Four Seasons." These works were composed while Vivaldi was in his twenties and thirties; in his latter years he concentrated mostly on opera, not always with much success. In 1740, apparently embittered by his lack of popularity in Venice, Vivaldi went to Vienna, where he died unknown and poverty-stricken one year later. After Vivaldi's death his work fell into neglect until Bach resuscitated it and wrote a set of variations on ten Vivaldi concerti, scoring them for organ and augmented orchestra. It was not until the twentieth century that he really came into his own, and much of the credit for his revival was due to intense campaigning on his behalf by the late expatriate American poet Ezra Pound and his violinist companion, Olga Rudge.

Another Venetian musician who was rediscovered in the twentieth century was Vivaldi's near contemporary, Tommaso Albinoni, author of twelve exquisite concerti and more than fifty operas. Albinoni's adagios are among the most profoundly moving in Venetian music. His Adagio in G Minor – often played as an independent piece – expresses a dignified, nostalgic sadness of extraordinary persuasiveness, the sadness of a proud people looking back upon a magnificent past from a vantage point of decay and uncertainty. Much the same feeling is conveyed by the works of the Marcello brothers, Alessandro and Benedetto, who composed a quantity of superb concerti at about the same time that Vivaldi and Albinoni were working. The Marcellos belonged to an ancient noble family that traced its ancestry back to Marcus Claudius Marcellus, the Roman general who fought in the Punic Wars. During its long history the family had given Venice many outstanding leaders, including a doge and several senators. The composers' father was a senator, writer, and violinist, and their mother was a painter and writer. First performances of Marcello works were held in the family palazzo, where Benedetto, a superb violinist, played on the never-to-be-surpassed instruments made in the Veneto workshops of Amati, Guarnieri, and Stradivari.

Talented as they were, neither Vivaldi, Albinoni, or the Marcellos enjoyed extraordinary popularity in their native city; that privilege was reserved for Baldassare Galuppi, who was unquestionably the most popular composer among his own people. The citizens of eighteenth-century Venice did not relish reminders of their city's decay. They preferred to be amused, and Galuppi took it upon himself to amuse them. His forte was the comic opera – the *opera buffa* – a spontaneous, bubbling, musical delight equivalent to the modern musical comedy. Galuppi wrote seventy of them, four a year, many to librettos by Goldoni and almost every one a popular success in Venice. His talent was as facile and fertile, although not as deep, as Vivaldi's – unfailingly smooth, blithe, and merry. In addition to *opera buffa,* he wrote many masses, concerti, oratorios, and served as director of music at St. Mark's. In time he became internationally famous, and when he died in 1785 Venice went into deep mourning. In its decline the republic wanted to laugh, and Galuppi had given them eighteen years of laughter. The city soon recovered its carefree spirit, however, for there were others capable of making Venetians laugh at their plight. Indeed, when the Lion of St. Mark finally collapsed, it was not amid dejection but buffoonery.

VI

The Long Sunset

Noblemen no longer wear their togas of office, the women have asses black from all the pinches they get; there is enough joking and luxury to make you vomit; religion is going down the drain," Angelo Maria Labia, poet, priest, and a member of a patrician Venetian family, lamented in a journal written in the mid-eighteenth century. Labia's Venice was a very strange place indeed; its peculiar type of decadence had no contemporary equivalents, and it is highly unlikely that anything remotely similar to it will appear again. By any commonly accepted standards, eighteenth-century Venice was a society gone mad.

It was called "the city of masks." Carnival lasted for six months, and people wore masks the entire time. The gambling that went on day and night was described by the Great Council — which eventually banned it — as "solemn, continuous, universal, violent." On one particular evening in 1762, the Abbé Grioni bet all his clothes on the turn of the wheel, lost, and returned to his monastery naked. Nuns wearing pearls and low-cut gowns fought among themselves for the honor of serving as mistress to a visiting papal nuncio. Ladies carried daggers and pistols for the management of their love affairs — which they preferred to be quick and without deep emotional involvement — and it was considered a disgrace for a married woman not to have a *cicisbèo,* or combination lover and gentleman-in-waiting.

By 1750, the city's rich were very, very rich — and her poor were very, very poor. Some patrician families had fortunes that amounted to hundreds of millions of dollars, lived in fifty-room palaces staffed with as many servants, owned as many as twelve gondolas, and maintained equally magnificent premises and appurtenances on the mainland. At the same time, the back *calli* of Venice teemed with beggars, cripples, and the horribly deformed. As the state grew poorer, it became more and more extravagant. The election of Doge Ruzzini in 1732 cost 34,473 lire, and the election, fifty-seven years later, of the man destined to be the last doge, cost 189,192 lire. Visiting potentates were given the most lavish welcomes in Europe by state officials once known for their selfless devotion to La Serenissima and now known for their almost universal corruption.

Industry was also in crisis. The Arsenale had employed 2,400 workers in 1645; by 1766 this number had dwindled to less than 1,500 — and these turned up only on payday, their jobs having become sinecures. Writing in 1780, Doge Paolo Renier observed: "We have no forces on land or sea. We have no alliances. We live wholly by luck." And yet despite her weakness and vulnerability, La Serenissima looked as if she had never suffered a defeat in her entire history, as if her empire were not only intact but destined to last forever. Most Venetian nobles acted as if Venice still ruled the entire Mediterranean Sea.

Relieved of the burdensome responsibilities of statecraft, the Great Council happily permitted the government to become more and more despotic. The Council of Three, now known as the State Inquisitors, assumed ever-increasing powers. These three patricians, two clad in black robes and one in red, ruled the republic from a small, elaborately decorated room on the second floor of the Doges' Palace. Their chief law-enforcement agent, Il Messer Grande, kept watch over the populace through an invisible army of spies.

It was, all things considered, a most peaceful century. With no wars to fight, with the lower and middle classes doing all the hard work, and with diminished political responsibilities, the Venetian nobleman was free — within the limits of his purse — to dedicate himself to what were euphemistically known as "his pleasures." The range of those pleasures was wide, for eighteenth-century Venice was a totally permissive society in which any behavior was condoned, as long as it was executed with style.

To be sure, not all Venetian nobles were wealthy enough to live the decadent life to the fullest. For one thing, the patrician class had dwindled considerably over the years, and many families had actually become extinct. Many others had become impoverished. Indeed, there were so many destitute noblemen in eighteenth-century Venice that they formed a fraternity known as I Barnabotti, named after the quarter in which they all lived on a subsistence allowance given them by the state. The number of families that could lead a life of pleasure probably numbered four hundred, but only two hundred of these were rich enough to indulge themselves to their hearts' contents.

The official passport to the new Venetian life of pleasure was the domino, a bizarre costume that combined a monstrous bird's-beak mask, a hood of velvet silk, and a three-cornered hat. The domino hid all signs of class and swept away all barriers. With the mask in place, one could do or say as one pleased. Priests in dominoes could conduct love affairs with impunity; working girls could sit next to patrician women at the gambling table. The Venetians were permitted to wear their dominoes six months of the year, from October to Christmas, and again from St. Stephan's Day, December 26, to Lent. During the six-month carnival, many nobles removed their masks only to go to bed. Commoners frequently did the same, and during carnival the two classes mixed as equals. It was the mask that finally brought democracy to Venice.

One place where nobles and plebians mixed freely together was the imposing structure known as the Ridotto, a gambling house that was located near the florid baroque Church of San Moisè, not far from Piazza San Marco. A veritable temple of chance in an age that worshiped money, the Ridotto's luxurious red and gold rooms were hung with stamped leather and illuminated by the finest crystal chandeliers from Murano.

In their stultifying idleness, Venetian noblemen carried gambling to inordinate extremes: they hazarded their clothes, their landed estates, even their wives — any one of which might find its way into the lap of a masked commoner. Many great patrician families were utterly ruined by gambling, and many commoners were vastly enriched. So serious a problem did gambling become that the Great Council voted to close the San Moisè Ridotto in 1774. Gambling did not cease, however, it simply went underground.

After gambling, extramarital sex was the most favored pastime of the settecento Venetians. For centuries Venetian women had been condemned to a straitlaced, secluded home life, little more than a harem existence, while the men restricted their sexual activities to their wives and their house servants. Then during the seventeenth century, standards of sexual morality began to relax — and by the middle of the following century, the sexual market was wide open. It has

Each chapter in Venice's long history has produced at least one major artist to record its passing: Carpaccio catalogued the city's rise to mercantile greatness; Canaletto recorded her years of golden affluence; and in the eighteenth century Giovanni Antonio Guardi detailed her slow decline. In the two interior scenes at right, Guardi's clear eye reveals the moral and spiritual corruption that was to spell the city's doom. Il Ridotto, the subject of the canvas at right, was a gambling den that functioned as a trysting place for people in all walks of Venetian life. Here titled aristocrats mingled with courtesans, and their wives with gigolos – all of whom hid their true identities behind masks. Another of Guardi's genre paintings (below) depicts Il Parlatorio, the reception salon of a Venetian nunnery of singularly ill-repute.

been said that in eighteenth-century Venice all women were courtesans. Absolute freedom reigned in the sexual sphere, and Venetian women made the most of it.

The key figures in the liberation of the Venetian woman were her tolerant husband and her *cicisbèo,* or recognized companion. After the first year of marriage, a patrician woman was free to choose her *cicisbèo* with the full consent of her husband. He had to be her social equal, a nobleman with a seat in the Great Council – and of course he had to be someone she actually liked. The *cicisbèo* attended his lady constantly, kissing her hand every time he met her, bearing her train, buying her opera tickets. He helped her into her gondola, called her servants for her, sat by her at dinner and the opera, shopped for her, shuffled cards for her, and waited for her while she did her toilette in the morning. Occasionally, but not always, he made love to her.

While the patrician wife was off frolicking with her *cicisbèo,* the patrician husband was more than likely frolicking with his love-of-the-moment at his "casino." This was a small love nest, usually decorated with Murano mirrors and suggestive frescoes, that the patrician maintained exclusively for the entertainment of his amours. The nobleman would take his love out to his casino in a covered gondola around noon, treat her to a sumptuous lunch laid out by a servant, then retire with her to the mirrored bedroom. Several hours later, the two would slip into the gondola and return to Venice from the mainland.

The quintessential Venetian libertine was Giovanni Jacopo Casanova de Seingalt, the son of a Venetian actor and a shoemaker's daughter. As he stated in his autobiography, *My Life and Adventures,* Casanova's

purpose was simply pleasure, and his greatest pleasure was sex, preferably with a new woman.

Like many libertines, Casanova also dabbled in magic and the occult, and this proved to be his undoing. Denunciations were issued from many quarters, his accusers calling him a "violater" and a "diabolist." The Council of Three began to watch him, and one July morning he awoke to find their agent in his house along with a contingent of police. He was taken by barge to the new prisons, where he was escorted over the Bridge of Sighs to the Doges' Palace. Dispensing with a trial, a council secretary ordered that he be taken to a cell in the stifling *piombi.* The cell was so small that Casanova could not stand up straight, the heat was unbearable, there was hardly any light, and "rats of fearful size walked unconcernedly about."

For fifteen months Casanova remained in the *piombi,* working the whole time on his escape. During one of his morning walks in the corridor outside his cell, he found a large iron bolt in a pile of rubbish. He sharpened the bolt on a piece of marble, using his spittle as a lubricant, and began digging his way out of the cell. Eventually he escaped onto the sloping roof of the Doges' Palace, slippery with the night mists. Opening a dormer window under the coping, he entered the palace — only to find that all exits were locked. At daybreak the great door above the Staircase of the Giants was opened, and he rushed out past startled guards. Dashing down the stairs, he fled across the Piazzetta to a gondola, in which he made his escape. He ultimately took a job as a librarian in Count von Waldstein's castle in Bohemia, where he wrote his memoirs. He died in 1798.

If we are to believe his memoirs, Casanova led the life of a libertine twelve months of the year; the rest of the population had to be content with the six-month carnival. During this long, publicly approved debauch, the city filled with wealthy tourists: wild young blades on allowances, middle-aged rakes, and aged roués trying to recapture their youth. They descended on the lagoon with only two thoughts in their heads – gambling and women. Noble ladies wearing black oval masks temporarily abandoned their husbands and *cicisbèi* to make themselves available to lecherous European lords, whose favorite place of assignation was the covered gondola. Noblemen wearing white, beaked masks preyed on tourists' wives and lured wealthy visitors into the Ridotto, where they gambled with "loans" from their guests. The cafes – there were two hundred of them, and many were open all night – became second homes for everyone.

At the height of this seasonal madness, Venetian nobles threw colossal parties for their most distinguished visitors. In 1784, for example, the Pisani family – owners of a pleasure villa on the Giudecca, a palace on the Grand Canal, a vast terra firma residence at Strà, as well as one hundred other residences in the Veneto – spent 200,000 lire – or roughly $3,000,000 – entertaining King Gustavus III of Sweden. During one wild party in Palazzo Labia, the head of the Labia family hurled all his gold plate out of his windows and into the Cannaregio Canal. These displays of staggering wealth could not hide the piles of filth that choked the *calli,* the rubbish floating in back canals, the scores of deformed and diseased beggars in the *campi,* or the poor Barnabotti in their tattered lace and faded silks. According to one eyewitness, St. Mark's was strewn with chicken coops at the time, and there were "noxious atmospheres emanating from the waters."

One would expect to see the arts founder in such a superficial and indulgent atmosphere, but as long as La Serenissima remained independent she continued to produce first-rate talents, and in the minor arts and engineering she managed to maintain her usual high standards. The eighteenth-century playwright Carlo Goldoni gave the world more than 150 comedies, some of which are still performed in Italy today. No contemporary Italian playwright could match the deftness of Goldoni's characterizations, the originality of his plots, or the density of his social context. Moreover, he was unfailingly funny, and his fat, awkward *borghesi* trying to act like elegant noblemen have become enduring symbols of eighteenth-century Venetian life.

Fortunately for future generations, the republic produced two first-rate painters to document her long decline – Pietro Longhi and Francesco Guardi. We need go no further than to the works of these artists to sense what La Serenissima was like during her last feeble years. Like so many great Venetian artists, Pietro Longhi began studying painting as a child. After two false starts, first as a religious painter and then as a Tiepolo-like decorator, he came into his own as a genre painter, executing small canvases of everyday life. Longhi's canvases are usually static compositions in which vapid, doll-like, blank-faced patrician women are seen surrounded by overattentive paramours, fawning priests, and periwigged husbands. The general lassitude of Longhi's subjects suggests how much vitality the Venetian aristocrats had lost by the mid-1700's.

The works of Pietro Longhi supplement Guardi's visual record of Venice's long, slow decline, offering unassailable evidence of the moral decay and sexual license that had become synonymous with Venice by the mid-eighteenth century. The four Longhi genre scenes at left treat separate events — a breakfast scene (far left), a visit from a pastry vendor, a concert, and (near left) the arrival of the first rhinoceros in Venice — but they state a single theme: the decadence of aristocratic life.

Judging from Longhi's portraits, the Venetian patricians had not only lost vitality, but also character — a loss that is particularly evident when a patrician and a commoner are portrayed in the same picture. Invariably the commoner emerges as the deeper personality; the patrician's face is a pallid blank, while the commoner's is etched with suffering and forbearance.

It remained to Francesco Guardi, the last Venetian artist of any importance, to express the decay and death of Venice in appropriately melancholy terms. Guardi's works bear witness to the death throes of a civilization, and as a result his canvases are, in a very real sense, a long and infinitely varied dirge. The artist was born only ten years after Longhi and fifteen years after Canaletto, yet there is a vast difference between the three painters' outlooks. Canaletto's and Longhi's works depict, in their separate ways, a decadent Venice but not a sad Venice. In Guardi's canvases the decay is unmistakably mournful; his eerie, nostalgic lagoonscapes are the visual counterparts of Albinoni's Adagio in G Minor.

Whereas Canaletto's conception of Venice became progressively clearer as he matured, Guardi's became increasingly nebulous and indistinct, prefiguring impressionism. Characters often seem to dissolve into or fuse with their surroundings. Colors are not steady, they flicker and vibrate. The outlines of buildings are soft and irregular. More important, Canaletto's Venice was, on the whole, a clean and orderly place; Guardi's is usually squalid and untidy. Weeds sprout from cornices, capitals, and windowsills; the façades of buildings are crumbling, flaking, decomposing; the piazzas and *campi* are filled with market stands, chicken coops, beggars, piles of rags, and trash; nets droop from bridges and boats; ruins sprout gardens of vines; and even the Venetians' dress, once so sumptuous, appears tawdry and ragged. No one seems to move briskly or purposefully in Guardi's Venice. All is languid, elusive. One senses a loss of energy, as if a thousand years of accumulated capital had finally been spent.

Occasionally Guardi does give us an echo of the old, triumphant Venice. The series of twelve paintings that commemorate the election of Alvise IV Mocenigo as doge are one example. Amid quivering colors and flickering lights, the new doge is crowned, acclaimed, and finally conducted across the lagoon in a gold and scarlet Bucentaur of almost hallucinatory splendor. And yet even in this festive series there are macabre touches: the black-hooded, white-beaked patricians who crowd the foreground in *The Reception of the New Doge in the Ducal Palace* seem to herald not a new beginning but a final end.

In addition to death and decay, solitude and emptiness also play an important role in Guardi's vision of Venice. Canaletto filled his lagoonscapes to overflowing with boats and shoreline buildings. Guardi, on the other hand, often portrayed the vast, solitary void of the lagoon, with perhaps only a gondola in the foreground. It has been said that Guardi, more than any other eighteenth-century Venetian artist, discovered the soul of Venice. If so, that soul was lonely, melancholy, and nostalgic, the soul of a great and glorious civilization that had lost everything but its memories — the soul of a people who "gave more to the world than the world is likely to repay." Although born in Venice, Guardi was able to look at his city in the detached man-

Even in decline, Venice clung to the pageantry that had earned her international renown during her heyday. For the coronation of Doge Alvise IV Mocenigo in 1703, for example, the aristocracy donned scarlet robes, assembled in the courtyard of the ducal palace (below), and cheered the investiture of an official whom the Ten had long since "reduced to a pageant." Appropriately enough, the pageantry associated with the closing of Venice's famed carnival is the theme of the Francesco Guardi work seen at right. From the central balcony of his palace, Doge Alvise IV surveys the crowds thronging the Piazzetta, decorated for the occasion with a towering temporary baldachin.

ner of a foreigner. What he saw was a dying civilization, and that is what he painted. His life and art were a finale, for with his death in 1793, four years before the death of the republic, came the death of Venetian art.

The situation in eighteenth-century Venice was a deceptive one because from 1718 to 1796 — seventy-eight long, self-indulgent years — there was peace both in Venice and along the boundaries of her shrunken empire. Thanks to the despotic Council of Three there was near-perfect law and order on the home islands, and foreigners observed that there was less crime in Venice than anywhere else in Europe. Furthermore, the revolutionary unrest that infected France and England was absent in Venice, where the patricians tenaciously defended the interests of the lower classes, and an easy familiarity prevailed among rich and poor, aristocrat and plebian. There was really no justification for friction of any kind, and amid such lovely surroundings complaints and resentments easily dissolved. So peaceful and unrevolutionary was La Serenissima in the eighteenth century that the ancien régime publicized it as "the aristocratic showcase of Europe," a place where revolution was thought to be impossible.

By the end of the eighteenth century, Venice's aristocratic government and social order stood in strident contrast to the new political ideas that the French Revolution was spreading throughout Europe. And yet those ideas did not find fertile soil in Venice. Naturally there had been alarm in the Senate when the Venetian ambassador's reports on the revolution arrived from Paris, but there had been no serious local repercussions. There had, of course, been some revolutionary murmurings. They never became a serious threat to the state, however, and even Napoleon's agents — who preached liberation to the ranks of the Barnabotti, to criminals, and to the unemployed — caused little disturbance.

All this meant little to Napoleon, who had a special loathing for ancient, aristocratic Venice. He called the patricians "a feeble-minded, mean-spirited people, unfit for liberty," and vowed to overthrow them. Descending into northern Italy in 1796 after humiliating the Austrians at Lodi, Napoleon occupied Cremona, Brescia, Bergamo, and Verona. The peasants in these provinces appealed to the Great Council for help, but none was forthcoming. And when mountaineers in the northern provinces rebelled, Napoleon falsely asserted that they had been encouraged by La Serenissima. He also accused Venice, rightly this time, of giving shelter to the brother of the murdered king of France, and of permitting the passage of Austrian troops through her territory. For these outrages and for the privilege of "bringing order to Venice," he demanded payment of a million francs per month for six months. The Great Council debated the matter and agreed to pay.

Napoleon next proposed an "alliance," which the Venetians also debated but took no action upon. On April 15, 1797, Easter Saturday, a day on which no business was ever transacted in Venice, Napoleon sent his aide-de-camp, General Andoche Junot, to the Great Council to discuss the terms of Venice's "liberation." The patricians hurriedly convened to receive him, and when Junot arrived in the vast, glittering Hall of the Great Council, they rose respectfully. The general sat down on the nuncio's chair, alongside the ducal throne, and immediately threatened the Venetian state with

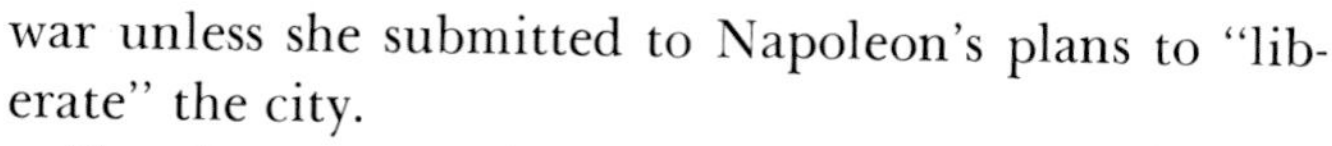

war unless she submitted to Napoleon's plans to "liberate" the city.

Napoleon was waiting impatiently for a pretext to attack, and on Easter Monday it came. On that same day the Veronese rose against the invaders, slaughtering many of the French troops bivouacked in their city. Shortly thereafter a French frigate was dispatched to Porto di Lido. As it approached the fort the Venetians opened fire, killing the frigate's commander. When news of the uprising at Verona and the death of his commander reached Napoleon, he flew into a rage. "I will have no more Doge!" he raved, "I will have no more Inquisitors! I will have no more Senate, no more Council of Ten; I will be an Attila to the State of Venice!" On May 1, 1797, he declared war.

When news of the emperor's declaration of war reached Venice, the patricians became panic-stricken and the common people poured into the piazza shouting "Viva San Marco! Viva San Marco!" Doge Lodovico Manin exclaimed, "Tonight we are not safe in our beds." Manin, a descendant of a family that had bought its way into the Golden Book in 1651, had been elected not because he was strong but because he was weak. The day he was elected he had burst into tears, fainted, refused dinner, and been carried to bed.

The Venetians could conceivably have given Napoleon a fight, for the Venetian navy, still a force to be reckoned with, was on the ready. Moreover, a regiment of well-trained *Schiavoni* ("Slavs") was stationed in Venice, and the perennially patriotic *arsenalòtti* were clamoring for blood. But Doge Manin's orders to his military commander were merely to "maintain the tranquility of the State and give ease and happiness to its subjects" — which the commander correctly interpreted as meaning to do nothing. When the French finally opened fire, the doge conferred with his advisers and decided to convene the Great Council. The Council met for the last time on May 12, 1797. Only 537 nobles were present — 63 short of a quorum. In a pathetic, barely audible speech, Doge Manin moved to abolish the five-hundred-year-old aristocratic government and institute a "government of the people." The Council's vote was overwhelmingly in favor of the motion. And when Manin went to bed that night he handed the white linen cap he wore under the ducal *corno* to his valet, muttering, "Take it way. We shall not be needing it anymore."

After the final meeting of the Great Council, placards were hung in Piazza San Marco to inform the people that the patricians had voluntarily renounced their hereditary rights, that the Council of Ten had been abolished, and that the three inquisitors had been arrested and sent to prison. The new government promised to rule in the name of liberty, fraternity, and equality. The Venetian people reacted to the news of their liberation with outrage and defiance. The nobles may have been weak, but the commoners were not, and they massed to protest the patricians' surrender. A riot broke out in Piazza San Marco, with gangs of *arsenalòtti* and sailors shouting "Viva San Marco! Viva San Marco!" and trying to storm the doors of the Doges' Palace. A few days later the Venetians allowed the French to liberate their city. After the French soldiers assembled in Piazza San Marco they sounded bugles, rolled drums, and broke into revolutionary songs. They then occupied all the key outposts.

The works of Giovanni Domenico Tiepolo share the grace but lack the vigor of those produced by his talented father — a telling comment on the whole course of Venetian history in the eighteenth century. Confining himself largely to subjects inspired by the fevered, lascivious atmosphere of his native city, the younger Tiepolo executed a series of views (left and right) of the white-clad clown that was the spirit of the six-month-long carnival.

Overleaf:
A stunningly colored, large-scale treatment of Giovanni Domenico Tiepolo's favorite subject — the nobility at play — focuses upon the most appealing and diverting aspects of carnival.

In early June, a Tree of Liberty was erected in Piazza San Marco between two statues representing freedom and equality. A great bonfire was lit beneath it, and as the fire rose up, illuminating the piazza, the ducal insignia — the doge's mantle, his robe, and the jeweled *corno* — were hurled into the flames, along with the Golden Book. After the burning, formal thanks was offered by the Venetian collaborators to "the glorious French nation and the immortal Bonaparte." With these symbolic acts and words, the Most Serene Republic of Venice ceased to exist. It had endured for more than one thousand years, longer than any republic in history.

The three masts in front of St. Mark's, which had once borne the flags of Cyprus, Crete, and the Morea, now flew the tricolor of revolutionary France. In the days following the burning of the ducal insignia and the Golden Book, coats of arms were stripped from patrician palaces and the inscription *The Rights of Man and Citizen* was placed over *Pax Tibi Marce* on most of the stone lions throughout the city. Subsequently, the four bronze horses were removed from the balcony of the basilica, and the Lion of St. Mark was taken down from its column on the Piazzetta; all five were then spirited away to Paris. During this same period, a mob of Barnabotti, petty criminals, and French sympathizers had broken into the Arsenale and attacked the Bucentaur, tearing gold leaf from its decks and smashing the figures that stood on either side of the doge's throne. The vessel was later broken up for firewood, and only a few fragments have survived.

On October 17, 1797, in accordance with the Treaty of Campoformido, all the Veneto including Venice was ceded to Austria. Eight years later, after the battle of Austerlitz, it was returned to France — only to be handed over to Austria again in 1814 by the Congress of Vienna as part of the general settlement following Waterloo. Visitors to the city during this unstable, demoralizing period were struck by the atmosphere of desolation. One British visitor observed, "Venice appeared to have lost all the life and light that had once rendered her so attractive."

The collapse of the Venetian Republic was a historical inevitability, for La Serenissima had been the victim of forces entirely beyond her control — the discovery of new trade routes to the East, the discovery of America, and the advent of the French Revolution, among others. She had also been victim of her own rigid political and social system, which made no allowance for the participation of the lower and middle classes in affairs of state.

During the short-lived French domination of Venice, Napoleon decimated all but a few members of the patrician class in one stroke by foreclosing the mortgages granted to nobles whose names were inscribed in the Golden Book. Napoleon also demolished the buildings bordering the west side of Piazza San Marco and erected the neoclassical Fabbrica Nuova in their place — a development which pleased no one. During the Austrian domination the conquerors built a railroad causeway from terra firma to Venice, made the French return the looted treasure of St. Mark's to Venice, imposed their own legal system on the Veneto, and instituted a harsh, authoritarian government by granting almost unlimited powers to the police. Simultaneously the Venetian lower and middle classes began to assert

themselves for the first time in history, spearheading a movement to liberate Venice from their hated oppressors. The leader of this movement was Daniele Manin, a lawyer of middle-class Jewish background.

Manin had adopted the name of the family that financed his education — the same Manins who had produced the last doge and one of the few patrician families that had not been beggared by Napoleon. Active in several revolutionary groups in the city, Manin was arrested by the Austrians for treason in 1848, a year in which revolutions erupted everywhere in Europe. Not long after the lawyer's incarceration, the people of Venice rose in his defense and demanded his release. When they obtained it, they entrusted Manin with the task of expelling the Austrians from the city and the lagoon.

Venice was once again proclaimed a republic, this time with Manin as president, and the city took a new lease on life. There was dancing in Piazza San Marco, fireworks over the lagoon, and balls in the great old palaces. Less than a year later, however, the Austrians regrouped and marched on Venice. For seventeen months, Daniele Manin and the Neapolitan general Guglielmo Pepe, leader of a relatively untrained army of merchants, shopkeepers, dockworkers, artisans, gondoliers and sailors, managed to stave off a vastly superior force of Austrians, who subjected the city to day and night bombardment. The Venetians dynamited the new railroad causeway near the mainland and erected cannon on the section still connected to the home islands. The Austrians retaliated by blockading the lagoon, causing famine and a cholera epidemic in Venice. But Manin, Pepe, and the Venetian people managed to hold out for several months. Finally, on August 24, 1849, the Austrians reoccupied the city.

The third Austrian domination lasted until Austria's defeat by the Prussians in 1866 at the conclusion of the Seven Week's War. During the intervening period, known as the Risorgimento, Venice played little or no part in the movement to unify Italy. Although she did not oppose the unification movement, she had always remained aloof from Italian politics, and she had never identified herself with the interests of the other Italian states. By 1866, Victor Emmanuel III, king of Sardinia, and Giuseppe Garibaldi had unified all of Italy except Venice and the Papal States, and at that point Venice was invited to join the new Kingdom of Italy. A plebescite was held, and the Venetians elected to join by a vote of 674,426 to 69.

Venice was subsequently made the capital of the Veneto, one of sixteen regions of the united Italian state, but her new status did not bring her new prosperity. The port of Trieste attracted much of her shipping, commerce and industry languished, and it was not until the last decade of the nineteenth century that her economy began to recover. This welcome resurgence was chiefly due to a rapid increase in tourism.

Artistically, nineteenth-century Venice was barren ground for the humiliated Venetians but exceedingly fertile territory for foreigners. Indeed, some of the greatest poetry and music of the nineteenth century was written by foreign artists in Venice. Venice had always been a haven for political exiles; it now became a haven for exiles from modern industrial civilization. The city exerted its most potent spell on artists from the most highly industrialized nations: Britain, Ger-

Venice's millennium of autonomy dissolved in the space of a few hours on May 12, 1797, as the once-mighty republic surrendered to Napoleon's troops. The emperor himself entered the city he had so frequently vilified in November 1807, at which time the municipal council erected a massive triumphal arch (left) that spanned the Grand Canal. Following the city's swift capitulation, Nero's bronze horses fell prey to yet another conqueror's acquisitiveness: the well-traveled chariot team was lowered from above the portal of St. Mark's (right) and transported to Paris, where the horses graced the Louvre for a decade before being returned.

many, and America. They went to Venice in search of what was being obliterated in their own countries — the romantic past, aristocratic culture, the picturesque.

In the vanguard of the British immigration was Lord Byron, who arrived shortly after the Congress of Vienna had handed the city back to the Austrians. He took an apartment in one of the Mocenigo palaces on the Grand Canal and remained several years. Robert Browning, another romantic exile infatuated by Venice, bought the opulent Ca' Rezzonico and lived in it until his death. "Open my heart and you will find graven on it: Italy," proclaims a plaque in his former study. The renowned art critic John Ruskin became the most extravagantly devoted lover of Venice in all its history. He lived on the Zattere, where he produced, among other works, three exhaustively researched volumes called *The Stones of Venice,* unquestionably the most complete description of the city ever written.

Among the many German sojourners in Venice, the most famous were Goethe, Nietzche, and Wagner. Goethe lived in a palace on the Grand Canal, took a very precocious interest in the biological and ecological problems of the lagoon, anticipated Byron by taking an equally precocious interest in a local countess, and wrote extensively about the city, maintaining that the first time he ever really *lived* was in Venice. Nietzche, a frequent visitor to Venice, once wrote: "When I try to think of a synonym for music, I think only of Venice." And whenever Wagner was suffering through a period of diminished creativity he would go to Venice — where his creative energy would suddenly return. He wrote the second act of *Tristan und Isolde,* with its sublime love duet, in the reception rooms of one of the Palazzi Giustiniani near Palazzo Foscari, and the cries of the city's gondoliers were supposedly the inspiration for the shepherds' pipe music that opens the third act of the same opera.

Americans too felt a special attraction to Venice. Dizzied by relentless change in their own country, where "progress" steadily eroded the past, American writers and artists of the nineteenth and early twentieth centuries saw Venice as a changeless continuity, an enchanted refuge of beauty and history in a world of burgeoning ugliness and brutality. One of the first American residents of Venice was the novelist William Dean Howells, who was given the post of United States consul in the city as a reward for writing a campaign biography of Abraham Lincoln. He was followed by Henry James, who first visited Venice in 1869.

During the following decades James paid countless return visits to the city. He usually stayed in a palace on the Grand Canal, and he always took copious notes on what he saw. Observing that "there is notoriously nothing new to be said on the subject [of Venice]," he proceeded to devote sixty-three pages of his *Italian Hours* to the city.

It would not be an exaggeration to say that during the nineteenth and twentieth centuries the foreign residents of Venice have made more news than the Venetians. Venetian civilization died in the year 1797. Since then Venice has gradually, almost imperceptibly, become an international city superimposed upon an Italian provincial town. From the standpoint of population, Venice is no bigger than Winston-Salem, North Carolina, yet it is the locus of three great international festivals — the Biennale of Contemporary Art,

the Biennale of Contemporary Music, and the International Film Festival — all of which lure major celebrities to the lagoon. It is also the home of several important international cultural institutions, such as the Giorgio Cini Foundation, which attracts scholars and congresses from all over the world. And according to the latest statistics, some two million tourists visit Venice each year — roughly twenty times the dwindling local population.

Notable events have occurred in twentieth-century Venice that had nothing to do with foreigners, of course. In 1902, for example, the Campanile of St. Mark's collapsed. The event was not unexpected, for nine hundred years of sirocco winds, bearing salt and Sahara stands, had taken their toll. Bricks had been abraded, cement had decomposed, and wooden piles had rotted. The 325-foot tower had been seen to sway, and on occasion a cluster of bricks would fall into the piazza. The city fathers became alarmed that if the Campanile did fall, it might destroy not only human life but also one or more of the surrounding buildings, depending on which way the wind was blowing and on which side of the structure the fatal crack appeared. Early in the morning on October 14, 1902, the piazza was closed, and statuary on the surrounding buildings was sandbagged. At 9:55 A.M. the Campanile fell. Luckily, it toppled into itself, disintegrating into an enormous pile of bricks, marble fragments, and dust. Three bells were irreparably damaged, but the Marangona, which had sounded reveille for six hundred years, survived intact, and the angel weather vane suffered only damaged wings. After the Campanile's collapse, the city council voted to bury the debris in the sea and place a funeral wreath on the waters. A new Campanile, a precise replica of the old, was completed on St. Mark's Day, 1912, exactly one thousand years after the original one had been begun.

During World War I, Venice was an important naval base and a center for operations against the hated Austrians, and it was therefore subjected to bombardment. As a precautionary measure, the bronze horses were removed from St. Mark's and the basilica was heaped with bags of seaweed and sand, but only the dome of the Scalzi church near the station suffered serious damage. In 1931, the ninth year of Mussolini's dictatorship, the much-disputed road causeway linking Venice and mainland Italy was completed, and the city thereby lost her last vestige of insularity.

Fortunately, World War II left Venice even less damaged than the first conflict had. The lagoon city headed the Nazis' list of proscribed bombing targets, and when the Germans occupied the city they did not harm a stone. Nor did the Allies, led by New Zealand troops, harm a stone when they liberated the city in 1945. The only artistic casualties of the war were some Tiepolo frescoes in the Palazzo Labia, which were cracked from the shock waves of a German ammunition ship that blew up in the lagoon.

Unquestionably the most important and repercussive event in twentieth-century Venice was the creation of the new industrial zone and port of Marghera on the western banks of the lagoon in 1917. The development was the brainchild of Giuseppe Volpi, Mussolini's minister of finance and later governor of Libya, and Count Vittorio Cini. The plan was to provide a source of steady employment for Venetian workers rendered

Weakened by wind and water erosion, the red brick Campanile of St. Mark's — a landmark to homeward-bound Venetian sailors since the sixteenth century — collapsed in 1902. Buffeted by sirocco winds, the 325-foot tower simply sank into itself (far left), scarcely damaging the buildings adjoining it in the process. Within a short time the resultant debris (near left) had been cleared away, and in 1912 — exactly one thousand years after the original campanile was begun — an exact replica of the fallen tower was dedicated by the city fathers.

jobless by the inexorable extinction of Venetian crafts and trades since the last days of the republic. If the sandbanks could be filled in, a harbor dredged, and petrochemical and other heavy-industry plants built, Venice could be resurrected as a great commercial port, thousands of jobs would open up for both workers and professionals, and the fabled lagoon city would enjoy a new renaissance.

Accordingly, Volpi's plan was approved in Rome, the western *barene* was filled in, a deep-water harbor was dredged, and before long tourists approaching Venice by land were greeted by one of the most infernally hideous industrial zones on the face of the earth, a sprawling tangle of pipes, tanks, and smokestacks pouring forth clouds of yellowish gas day and night. At first, Volpi's Marghera was hailed as the solution to the problem of Venice's future. But after World War II, when Marghera was badly bombed and had to be rebuilt, many people — including Volpi's own children — began to feel that Marghera, far from solving Venice's problems, was creating worse ones. For one thing, the industries, most of whose administrative headquarters were in Milan and Turin, were employing primarily non-Venetian executives and workers. For another, filling in the *barene* had destroyed one of the lagoon's natural safety devices and had thereby increased the danger of flooding from high water. Sulfuric pollution from the petrochemical plants was corroding Venice's most priceless artistic treasures, and pumping out fresh water for industrial cooling from beneath the lagoon's floor was removing a natural cushion and causing the entire area to sink. While the other cities of northern Italy were enjoying an unprecedented economic boom, Venice, formerly the richest city in all Italy, was in the doldrums — poorer in comparison to her neighbors than she had ever been.

During her fifteen-hundred-year history, Venice, the refuge from barbarism, the preserver and rebuilder of civilization, had survived in succession, the Goths, the Lombards, the Byzantines, the Franks, the Swabians, the Genoese, the Milanese, the papacy, the Turks, Spain, herself, France, and the Austrians. Now, in the mid-twentieth century, in the most "progressive" era of mankind, the solution to her problems was threatening to become her final undoing, the coup de grace that even Napoleon had been incapable of administering.

VII

Venice Imperiled

Around 10:00 P.M. on the evening of November 3, 1966, water began to spill over the Riva degli Schiavoni, flow through the Piazzetta, and pour into Piazza San Marco. No one in Venice was overly alarmed by this particular high tide, for during the fall and winter seasons such tides often rise above the level of the old foundations and spill into the city's streets and squares. When the tide ebbed, the waters would recede as usual, perhaps leaving an oar or a crate stranded in front of St. Mark's.

Ebb tide was supposed to begin about five o'clock on the morning of November 4. Shortly after that hour observers did note a slight decrease in the water level throughout the city – but nothing resembling a full-scale retreat. By 7:00 A.M. it was apparent that the waters were not going to recede. This was extremely alarming because the next high tide was only five hours away. When it came, shortly after noon, the already swollen waters rose even more, well above the level reached earlier that morning. An unusually powerful sirocco was blowing from the south, accompanied by heavy rains. Soon the lagoon was no longer just spilling into the city, it was lashing into it, surging into it. Huge waves were breaking against the columns of St. Theodore and St. Mark, and even those parts of the city normally immune to *acqua alta*, or "high water," were going under. By midafternoon all telephones were out of order, electricity had failed, most of the gas lines were disrupted, all furnaces were quenched, all ground-floor stores and dwellings were flooded, and the water was so deep in the *campi* and *calli* that it was impossible to move about the city except by boat.

The local radio station informed distressed Venetians that ebb tide was expected around 6:00 P.M. and that then the water would recede. Six o'clock arrived, and to everyone's dismay and terror the water did not recede, it rose. What the radio announcer had failed to tell the people was that the *murazzi*, the great sea walls along the Lido, had given way and that the full might of the Adriatic, driven by gale-force winds, had been unleashed upon the lagoon. The islands of Cavallino, Burano, Vignolo, and Sant' Erasmo were already inundated, and hundreds of bathing establishments and hotels along the Lido had been destroyed.

By 8:00 P.M. the Venetians, marooned in their unlighted, unheated homes, realized that this was not just another *acqua alta*, this was a major disaster; this might even be the end of Venice. The water had risen six and a half feet above normal, the highest level in recorded history, and it showed no signs of receding. All was in darkness. Then suddenly, shortly after 9:00 P.M., the water began receding – not slowly as it usually did, but rapidly, violently, with the abrupt force of a miracle. Looking out their windows, the Venetians vaguely saw and emphatically heard the water rushing down the canals and *calli* as if some sea god had pulled a stopper from the floor of St. Mark's basin and the whole lagoon were suddenly being drained.

By midnight Venice was above water and the Venetians were out inspecting the havoc by candlelight. To some the scene looked like a gigantic funeral. Skeletons of boats and gondolas blocked the *calli*. Great black smears of fuel oil besmirched walls and pavements. Mattresses, chairs, tables, and garbage were scattered everywhere; dead pigeons, rats, and cats floated in the canals. Debris choked every basement, every ground

floor. Almost every store in the city had been devastated, as had hundreds of artisans' workshops. Thousands of furnaces were irreparably damaged, thousands of library books destroyed. Furniture had been ruined in flooded houses, public documents in lawyers' offices. Sixteen thousand ground-floor residents had been deprived of all their possessions, and damage estimates ranged as high as $64,000,000. The injury done to statues, paintings, frescoes, palaces, and churches was all but incalculable.

The flood of November 3–4, 1966, was the result of a coincidence of forces and events not likely to occur again in a single twenty-four-hour period for many years. The exceptionally high tides were not themselves unusual for November, but the periodic oscillatory motion of the Adriatic had piled up an exceptionally large mass of water in the sea's northern end. In addition, a furious sirocco was blowing from the south, driving these already high waters before it. And a heavy rain was falling, swelling the rivers that emptied into the lagoon.

As unusual as this coincidence of forces was, there can be little doubt that their cumulative effect was intensified by processes that have been going on in Venice and the lagoon over the last five decades — and there is even less doubt that if present trends are allowed to continue, future *acque alte,* even if they are not as high or as sustained as the one of 1966, will be even more disastrous for Venice, hastening what appears to be the city's certain death by drowning within the next fifty to seventy-five years.

For it is an undeniable fact that Venice today is dying, both physically and spiritually. In the first place, the entire city, including the mainland industrial and residential zones of Marghera and Mestre, is sinking into the lagoon. Some areas are subsiding faster than others (parts of St. Mark's have sunk as many as six inches in the past sixty years), but the median subsidence is about five millimeters a year. Simultaneously, the level of the Adriatic is rising about one and a half millimeters a year due to the thawing of the polar ice caps. This makes the effective subsidence six and a half millimeters, or roughly one quarter of an inch annually. At this rate, which will probably accelerate, much of Venice will be uninhabitable in seventy-five years, and in a hundred and fifty years only scuba divers will be able to visit it.

In the second place, the city is decaying from a combination of neglect, erosion, and pollution. Rotted piles underneath buildings, *fondamenti* and *campi* have not been replaced, and during high tide or when motorboats churn up the canals, water rises above the hard stone foundations of buildings and seeps into salt-saturated masonry, sucking out loosened cement, plaster, and bricks. Abandoned apartment houses are allowed to decay, and the owners of monumental palaces, confronted with the high cost of maintaining their establishments, generally prefer to let them deteriorate rather than underwrite their upkeep. As a result, 40 per cent of Venice's buildings are uninhabitable, and 75 per cent have inadequate plumbing. Add to this neglect the damage caused by air pollution, and an already serious situation becomes a disastrous one.

Until recently, petrochemical emissions from Marghera, especially during July and August, combined with motorboat exhaust fumes and smoke from the

burning of low-grade fuel oils, poured 15,000 tons of sulfuric acid into the air over the city every year. These pollutants, along with the corrosive guano of Venice's 50,000 pigeons, decompose marble with high carbon content, causing cornices to crumble and delicately wrought statuary to disintegrate. Already 35 per cent of Venice's outdoor sculpture is badly damaged, and it is estimated that under present conditions Venice could lose the greater part of her artistic face in forty years.

Even more serious, Venice is being abandoned by its own citizens. Since 1951 the city's population has dropped from 192,000 to 131,000; between 1960 and 1972 alone, 40,000 Venetians emigrated to Mestre and Marghera. In the last analysis, the smog and monotony of the mainland industrial zones have proved preferable to the exorbitant rents Venetians were obliged to pay for decaying, damp, unheated, and frequently flooded living quarters. Most serious of all, Venice is dying spiritually. Mestre and Marghera have drawn away almost all of Venice's commerce and industry, and so the Venetians have nothing left to do but serve tourists. This, for a people who once dominated the Mediterranean, has been profoundly demoralizing.

Who, or what, is to blame for this critical situation? One answer, of course, is that no one is really to blame for the city's current plight, for the imminent death of Venice may be seen as the inevitable conclusion of a chain of calamities that began in the late fifteenth century with the discovery of America and new trade routes to the Orient. Others, who claim that these events had run their course by the time of the fall of the republic, note that Venice acquired a new identity in the nineteenth century, following her incorporation into the Italian national state, and they therefore insist that a different judgment is necessary.

In this light many historians will not be able to resist pinning the blame for the decay of Venice squarely upon Italian and Venetian business and political leaders, especially those on the board of directors of the major industries in Marghera. For it was during the crucial years of Italy's post-World War II industrial renaissance that a combination of narrow egotism, inertia, lack of vision, petty rivalry, outright greed, bureaucratic absurdity, and plain bungling set the stage for the deterioration and depopulation of Venice.

To understand the contemporary crisis in Venice it is important to have some understanding of the geography and the hydraulics of the Venetian lagoon. Lagoons are formed wherever large rivers empty into a sea, and they represent a natural interaction between land and water. The Venetian lagoon is a typical one, formed by the effluence of three large rivers that empty into the Adriatic. It is composed of a series of interlocking tidal basins studded with islands and mud flats, and it has three *porti*, or "accesses," to the sea. Like the sea, these tidal basins experience two high tides and two low tides very day. During high tide the sea rushes in through the three *porti* and pours into the individual basins; then during ebb tide it flows back out through the *porti* into the Adriatic, carrying refuse with it. The motion of water within each basin is circular, and because of this scouring action Venice has had no need of sewers. Thanks to the tides, the canals are flushed clean twice daily.

For almost fifteen centuries the equilibrium of the lagoon was maintained in favor of Venice. When the

Since the beginning of her history, Venice has been compelled to coexist with the sea. The tides that regularly flush out her canals and purify the lagoon have, with increasing regularity, doubled or trebled in size and inundated the low-lying areas of the city (far left). The curse of acqua alta, *"high water," is an old and familiar one to the Venetians; the curse of industrial pollution is relatively new. Moreover, the wind-propelled argosies that once plied the lagoon have been replaced by tankers belching soot and fumes (near left), and many of the city's gondolas have been replaced by churning* vaporetti. *In combination with the nearby industrial zone of Marghera, they are fouling the city's air and eroding her foundations at an alarming rate. To compound Venice's agony,* acque alte *now threaten as never before. In 1966, for instance, a particularly fierce floodtide broke over Venice, sundering the city's very foundations (right).*

city was threatened by natural forces — the silt of rivers, the raging of the sea — La Serenissima took proper measures to restore the equilibrium. But in 1917, with the creation of Marghera, a man-made force began to upset the equilibrium of the lagoon, and thus far next to nothing has been done to restore the balance. The industrial complex at Marghera has disturbed that balance in three ways. First, the filling in of the *barene,* or tidal flats, to accommodate the factories has created artificial barriers to the free flow of water within the lagoon. In the past, high tides spilled slowly out across the *barene,* and the ebb tide flowed slowly back over it. The violence of both tides was thus cushioned, diffused, and absorbed over a vast expanse of mud and reeds. After the tidelands were reclaimed, these high tides were repulsed by the landfill, and unusually large masses of water built up in mid-lagoon, where they met the onrushing tide — often causing unusually high water in Venice.

Second, the extraction of fresh water from the lagoon's subsoil for industrial consumption in Marghera has contributed substantially to the subsidence of much of the lagoon floor, including that beneath Venice itself. And third, the dredging of the deep-water tanker channel and harbor — an operation that also involved the widening of the Malamocco entrance to the lagoon — has enabled water as well as tankers to enter the lagoon more easily. As a result, when high tide and high south winds coincide, the Adriatic swells the lagoon more rapidly than before. Concomitantly, the admission of deep-water tankers into the lagoon — many of which enter the Porto di Lido, steam through St. Mark's basin, and head for Marghera down the Giudecca Canal — has furthered the erosion of palace foundations through violent wave action. It goes without saying that the more than six thousand tankers that navigate the Venetian lagoon annually also contribute substantially to the city's water pollution problem.

Marghera's murderous effect on Venice does not stop with upsetting the natural equilibrium of the lagoon, however, for Giuseppe Volpi's solution to the problem of Venice's lagging economy has also resulted in the financial and demographic impoverishment of the city. Many of the Venetians who found employment in Marghera after the war have left Venice to live in Mestre, and these workers naturally spend most of their salaries in Mestre, not Venice. Most of Marghera's executives are legal residents of Piedmont and Lombardy who have been sent to Marghera by their companies — and hence the municipality of Venice does not collect taxes from them. For the most part, they live in Mestre and spend their salaries in Mestre. To compound the disaster, few of the Marghera industries belong to Venetians, and few Venetians own stock in them, so practically none of Marghera's profits wind up in Venice either.

Over the last two decades both the national government and the government of Venice itself have become accomplices to this crime. Since most of greater Venice's inhabitants now live in Mestre and Marghera, the mayors of Venice, ever vigilant for votes, have tended to dedicate more time and money to terra firma than to the islands. Likewise, since the money in the area is generated by heavy industry in Marghera, the national government, closely allied with big business, has tended to identify more with the needs of Marghera's powerful

Marble cancer, the apparently irreversible corrosion that has already disfigured statuary throughout Venice, threatens to engulf every piece of carved stone in the city unless a means is found to halt its spread. Acetic pigeon guano, sulphur dioxide fumes from the smokestacks of Marghera, and damp sea air have abetted and accelerated the process — which has already gnawed at the statues at right.

corporations than with the sinking queen of the lagoon.

State and local authorities profess a keen interest in saving and restoring Venice's monumental palaces. Yet if the owner of a palace on the Grand Canal does restore his building he is heavily taxed for his pains, whereas new buildings are not taxed for twenty-five years. One of the results of this policy, which obviously favors new housing developments in Mestre-Marghera, has been to promote the construction of jarringly modern buildings in the center of the old city. The Savings Bank of Venice, for instance, chose to build a new, uninspired bank and administrative headquarters rather than restore any of several magnificent old palaces — a farsighted course chosen by the national television network, now housed in the restored Palazzo Labia, and by the Bank of Italy, with offices in the renovated Palazzo Manin.

Thanks to worldwide interest and concern generated by the flood of 1966, several high-ranking Italian officials introduced measures in parliament to safeguard Venice against subsidence, decay, and inundation. A loan of 250 billion lire (roughly $400,000,000) was obtained from an international consortium of banks to support a plan for the reclamation and restoration of the entire city. International concern over Venice's plight proved so great that the Italians encountered no difficulties in raising the money; in fact, some banks that were not approached initially actually pleaded to be allowed to participate. Once the money was guaranteed, fund-raiser Mario Ferrari-Aggradi, who was a member of the Chamber of Deputies from Venice and the newly appointed minister of public works, introduced a bill to safeguard Venice. Furious squabbling broke out almost immediately over who would spend the 250 billion lire. Should the loan go to the municipality of Venice, the Veneto region, the national government, or to a special high commission? Ferrari-Aggradi's original bill provided for the national government to oversee the administration of the funds, but this was violently opposed by the Venetian city council, led by the mayor, who felt that their competence to administer the funds was being questioned. After seemingly endless bickering, a compromise was reached that allowed all three governments — municipal, regional, and national — to share in spending the allocated money.

Article I of the revised bill states reassuringly that the Republic of Italy "guarantees the safeguarding of Venice's historic center and its archeological and artistic patrimony, as well as the integrity of its landscape, and the hydrological equilibrium of the lagoon," and that it will undertake "to protect the city and the lagoon from air and water pollution and assure the socio-economic vitality of the area in the context of the general development of the region." The bill also provides for the establishment of a high commission to safeguard Venice. It will be up to this group to decide exactly how the 250 billion lire will be spent within the guidelines established by the bill.

As the bill now stands, Rome is to spend 87 billion lire on the defense of the lagoon and the protection of the environment, a provision that may include the installation of three movable dikes to seal off the entrances to the lagoon during abnormally high tides. The Veneto will receive 58 billion lire to construct a new aqueduct and sewage system and to help home-

owners transform their heating systems from oil to gas. The municipality will get some 100 billion lire for the restoration of monumental palaces, bridges, and sculptures in Venice itself. The remaining 5 billion lire is to be spent by all three branches of government on research and plans.

The movable dikes have been authoritatively proposed by Professor Roberto Frassetto, director of a laboratory that has been set up for the study of the hydrodynamics of the lagoon, an undertaking subsidized by Italy's prestigious National Research Council. These dikes would function on a computerized, six-hour warning system, and according to experts they would definitely prevent floods in Venice. However, the periodic closing of the three entrances to the lagoon could conceivably interrupt the free circulation of water within the lagoon, which is why the new sewage system has to be installed as well. Once in service, it will obviate the city's dependence upon the tides to flush the lagoon twice daily. Because it is thought that the removal of underground water is the principal cause of the subsidence of the lagoon's subsoil, the aqueduct that is to be built by the Veneto government is an equally important provision of the safeguard bill.

The proposal to construct a dike across the Malamocco entrance to the lagoon has been a source of violent controversy — largely because the deep-water canal cut through Malamocco in the 1960's was dredged specifically to accommodate large tankers bound for the port of Marghera. It has been estimated that it will be necessary to close the Malamocco gate for only 209 hours each year, but Marghera's industrial lobby has nonetheless prevented approval of the Malamocco dike. Consequently, the bill, which was approved by the Senate in December 1971, was worded in such a way as to leave the critical question of the Malamocco dike unanswered.

While Italian politicians have been arguing over how the funds allocated for the relief of Venice should be spent, help from private individuals and foundations has rained on beleaguered Venice from every quarter of the globe, including Italy itself. Long before the great flood of 1966 focused the world's attention on the plight of Venice, the Italian industrialist Count Vittorio Cini, co-founder of the Marghera industrial zone, privately undertook the restoration of the island of San Giorgio Maggiore, and in particular the Benedictine monastery built there by Longhena and Palladio. There, in 1951, he established the Giorgio Cini Foundation as a memorial to his son. The result was one of the finest restorations ever completed in Italy. The beautifully appointed foundation, which contains the School of San Giorgio for the study of Venetian civilization among its many divisions, attracts scholars and congresses from all over the world and is regarded as a model of its kind.

The Cini Foundation and the aforementioned Palazzo Labia, restored by Italy's state-owned radio and television network, are examples of what enlightened Italians did to save Venice before the flood of 1966. After the flood, Italian contributions were second only to those of the United States. The Italian government, which donated $50,000,000 in emergency relief aid shortly after the 1966 flood, is also underwriting Professor Frassetto's laboratory on San Giorgio at a cost of $1,000,000 a year.

In the wake of the disastrous acqua alta *that hit Venice in November 1966, makeshift workshops were set up to restore and refurbish the scores of major artworks that had been damaged by the high water. At Pontecasale (left), a permanent restoration center recently established on the mainland, canvas backing is glued onto a frayed and weakened painting to give it added support. Among the art treasures that were salvaged through the painstaking efforts of numerous international groups are Veneziano's* Virgin and Child, *being retouched at near right, and a work by the eighteenth-century artist Piazzetta, undergoing cleaning at far right.*

The Italians have also made major contributions toward restoring damaged works of art. After the flood of 1966 the superintendent of fine arts and museums for the Veneto, Professor Francesco Valcanover, set up a restoration center and laboratory in the empty Church of San Gregorio. Today two more restoration centers have been established, one for small canvases in the Church of San Toma, and a mobile one for exceptionally large works at the Scuola di San Rocco.

Italy's national conservation society, Italia Nostra, has also made vital contributions toward rescuing Venice, including the restoration of Verrocchio's magnificent monument of Colleoni. Until recently the Venice chapter of Italia Nostra was headed by Countess Anna Maria Cicogna Volpi, daughter of the co-founder of Marghera. An indefatigable fighter for Venice, Countess Volpi was partly responsible for getting the municipality to forbid the pumping of fresh water from the city's innumerable artesian wells and to forbid the burning of low-cost fuel oils in the city's furnaces. She also pressured the city fathers into requiring that Marghera's industries attach antipollution filters to factory smokestacks, and she helped persuade the government to force the industrial consortium to halt its plans for the third industrial zone in Marghera.

By far the largest contributions to the various programs to restore Venice have come from the United States, although British, French, and German committees have also contributed substantial sums. To date the most significant restorations have been financed and carried out by the Venice Committee of the International Fund for Monuments. These have included the restoration of the façade of Ca' d'Oro and the vast Tintoretto cycle in the Scuola di San Rocco, the restoration of the Scuola dei Carmini, and the restoration of numerous churches.

What the future holds for Venice is somewhat hard to envision, but one thing is certain: if the city is to be truly saved, she must find a purpose more noble and creative than mass tourism. Venice today is little more than a vast museum through whose creaking turnstiles pass some two million visitors each year. During the height of the summer season, the city is choked with tourists; during the off-season, Venetian life is monotonous and desultory. After the museums close, there is almost nothing for visitors to do but go to a cafe in Piazza San Marco and listen to a string orchestra play a mournful rendition of "Arrivederci Roma." The great festivals are not what they used to be. The Biennale of Contemporary Art, for example, no longer has a monopoly on its traditional function, that of acquainting artists of all countries with current developments in contemporary art.

As for the city's social life — and social life was once Venice's greatest attraction — it, too, is moribund. Most of the great patrician families are extinct, and most of those that have survived lack sufficient means to entertain on anything like the old grand scale. Furthermore, most of the Venetian young have fled. According to a recent survey, if depopulation continues at the present rate, by 1981 there will be only 80,000 inhabitants left in Venice — and of these, 44,000 will be over the age of forty-five. If the present rate and type of depopulation continues unchecked until 1991, the city will be little more than a retirement village periodically inundated by tourists.

The solution to Venice's social, economic, and psychic ills must grow out of an understanding of what it is that Venice still has to offer the world, for in spite of decay and depopulation the city still offers certain unique advantages that cannot be duplicated elsewhere. It was not for nothing that the internationally renowned French architect Le Corbusier considered Venice the most ideally structured city in the world, the justification of his most cherished theories. In contrast to most modern cities, Venice encourages social contact among its inhabitants and offers them living on a truly human scale. The city is composed of a series of interconnected nuclei, each with its own square, or *campiello,* which serves as a meeting place for the neighborhood. Several of these in turn form a larger quarter with a larger square, or *campo,* the meeting place for the entire quarter. And all the quarters in turn form Venice, with its meeting place for the whole city, Piazza San Marco. It is readily apparent to even the most casual observer that the residents of each nucleus enjoy a very strong sense of community. This sense of community is heightened by easy access to all sections. Venice is so laid out that almost any point in the city can be reached on foot in twenty to thirty minutes from the Rialto. And of course there are no cars, which means no parking problems, no exhaust fumes, no stoplights, no traffic, and little noise.

There is little need to dwell on Venice's obvious artistic worth, but a few statistics might be illuminating. According to a comprehensive UNESCO study, there are 847 frescoes and 4,000 bas-reliefs and sculptures of unusual artistic worth in Venice, plus 700 monumental palaces built before the fall of the republic, 105 churches and 20 *scuole* of outstanding architectural merit, and at least 200 oil paintings of the first rank. In short, Venice is nothing less than the largest and richest single depository of works of art in the world, and the largest single concentration of pre-nineteenth-century buildings in the world. No city the size of Venice has left a legacy of comparable aesthetic and educative value.

The question now is how to take advantage of these unique assets, how to develop activities that would be best served by the urban values Venice possesses. It is generally agreed that Venice is an ideal setting for learning, study, and the exchange of ideas, and many have suggested that the city be made into an *isola di studi,* an "island of studies" attracting students, educators, researchers, writers, scientists, and artists from all over the world. Some progress has in fact already been made in this direction: the Cini Foundation has for the past twenty years been attracting scholarly congresses to its facilities on the island of San Giorgio Maggiore, and in 1969 the International University of Art was founded in Venice. More recently a German institute was opened and the University of Venice was expanded. Plans are also under way to create a British-American institute that would serve as a base in Venice for American and British universities, providing them with lecture halls, study rooms, and equipment.

It is the opinion of some that once Venice has been safeguarded physically, the city will gradually come back to life as an important administrative and commercial center as well as a cultural and tourist center. As the administrative capital of the increasingly prosperous Veneto region, with many of Venice's monu-

Her plight the subject of international concern and her future as beclouded as her polluted canals, Venice endures. Once thought to be the loveliest city ever created, she is now a picture of gentle decay, the memory of her past glories fast fading. As Byron wrote with remarkable prescience in 1812:

> *Oh Venice, Venice, when thy marble walls*
> *Are level with the waters. . .*
> *What should thy sons do?*
> *Anything but weep:*
> *And yet they only murmur in their sleep.*

mental palaces taken over by the regional government, there would be a sharp increase in government jobs for Venetians. By means of a more enlightened tax policy, Venice could revive as a great commercial, as opposed to industrial, port.

In the purely pragmatic view held by many others, however, there is little or no chance Venice will ever recover anything resembling her former status. If the city is to become a world center again — whether educational, cultural, or political — she will need much more than the 250 billion lire already raised on her behalf. She will need broad, concerted leadership from many segments of Italian society — and it is questionable whether modern Italy's profit-oriented consumer society and shaky coalition government is capable of providing that aid and guidance.

To be realistic, then, we must recognize that if Venice is to be saved by the Italians its rescue must be financially profitable for them. They will probably try to have their cake and eat it too, by preserving Venice for the tourists while simultaneously encouraging further industrial expansion in Marghera. In this way Venice will, after a fashion, be saved. Significant steps have, in fact, already been taken to realize these seemingly incompatible ends. On September 4, 1972, the special legislation to safeguard Venice already passed by the Italian Senate was introduced into the Chamber of Deputies, the parliament's lower house. Assuming that the bill will be passed, it will be only a matter of time before the movable dikes are installed, the aqueducts and sewers built, and most of the monumental palaces and churches restored. At the same time, however, Montecatini-Edison, one of Italy's largest industrial concerns, has recently invested 244 billion lire in its Marghera plant. Thus we may assume that tourists will continue to flood the city, and that Marghera will continue to pollute the air and water as before.

Physically, at least, Venice will have been saved. As for her soul, that no one is capable of restoring. For the real death of Venice occurred 175 years ago, on that early June day when a great bonfire was lit under the Tree of Liberty and the ducal insignia and the Golden Book were hurled into the flames.

But although the pride and dignity of La Serenissima can never be revived, the example of Venice will endure as a permanent source of inspiration for all men. That example was one of consummate heroism — the triumph of a people who turned barren mudflats into a supreme work of beauty, who turned a nightmare of devastation and defeat into a towering victory of the human spirit.

Book cover created for the coronation of Doge Alvise IV Mocenigo in 1703

VENICE
IN LITERATURE

RESTLESS ROMANTICS

Lord Byron's short life had a profound impact upon young Englishmen of his generation. The intense and melancholy poet succumbed to fever in 1824 while fighting for Greek independence, but his spirit continued to influence countless contemporaries. The fourth canto of Childe Harold's Pilgrimage, *a fictionalized account of Byron's spiritual quest across Europe, was composed in Italy.*

I stood in Venice on the Bridge of Sighs,
A palace and a prison on each hand;
I saw from out the wave her structures rise
As from the stroke of the enchanter's wand:
A thousand years their cloudy wings expand
Around me, and a dying glory smiles
O'er the far times when many a subject land
Looked to the winged Lion's marble piles,
Where Venice sate in state, throned on her hundred isles!

II

She looks a sea Cybele, fresh from ocean,
Rising with her tiara of proud towers
At airy distance, with majestic motion,
A ruler of the waters and their powers:
And such she was; – her daughters had their dowers
From spoils of nations, and the exhaustless East
Poured in her lap all gems in sparkling showers.
In purple was she robed, and of her feast
Monarchs partook, and deemed their dignity increased.

III

In Venice Tasso's echoes are no more,
And silent rows the songless gondolier;
Her palaces are crumbling to the shore,
And music meets not always now the ear:
Those days are gone – but beauty still is here.
States fall, arts fade – but Nature doth not die,
Nor yet forget how Venice once was dear,
The pleasant place of all festivity,
The revel of the earth, the masque of Italy!

IV

But unto us she hath a spell beyond
Her name in story, and her long array
Of mighty shadows, whose dim forms despond
Above the dogeless city's vanished sway:
Ours is a trophy which will not decay
With the Rialto; Shylock and the Moor,
And Pierre, cannot be swept or worn away –
The keystones of the arch! though all were o'er,
For us repeopled were the solitary shore. . . .

XI

The spouseless Adriatic mourns her lord;
And, annual marriage now no more renewed,
The Bucentaur lies rotting unrestored,
Neglected garment of her widowhood!
Saint Mark yet sees his lion where he stood

Arch of the Clock Tower in the Piazza San Marco; from a series of Venetian sketches (pp. 138–60) by Francesco Guardi

Stand, but in mockery of his withered power,
Over the proud Place where an emperor sued,
And monarchs gazed and envied in the hour
When Venice was a queen with an unequalled dower. . . .

XIII

Before Saint Mark still glow his steeds of brass,
Their gilded collars glittering in the sun;
But is not Doria's menace come to pass?
Are they not *bridled?* — Venice, lost and won,
Her thirteen hundred years of freedom done,
Sinks, like a seaweed, into whence she rose!
Better be whelmed beneath the waves, and shun,
Even in destruction's depth, her foreign foes,
From whom submission wrings an infamous repose. . . .

XXV

But my soul wanders; I demand it back
To meditate amongst decay, and stand
A ruin amidst ruins; there to track
Fallen states and buried greatness, o'er a land
Which *was* the mightiest in its old command,
And *is* the loveliest, and must ever be
The master-mould of Nature's heavenly hand,
Wherein were cast the heroic and the free,
The beautiful, the brave, the lords of earth and sea.

LORD BYRON
Childe Harold's Pilgrimage, 1817

In Germany, as in England, the creative minds of the late eighteenth and early nineteenth centuries were captivated by Romanticism's defiant worship of nature and emotion. The publication of The Sorrows of Young Werther *sparked a wave of suicides among impressionable youths inspired by the hero's tragic fate. Its author, Johann Wolfgang von Goethe, a leader of the "Sturm und Drang" literary movement that prefigured German Romanticism, was acutely attuned to his times. The young poet and novelist's account of his visit to Venice in 1786 reveals another aspect of his lyrical sensitivity.*

Now it stood written on my page in the Book of Fate, that on the evening of the 28th of September, by 5 o'clock, German time, I should see Venice for the first time, as I passed from the Brenta into the lagunes, and that, soon afterwards, I should actually enter and visit this strange island-city, this heaven-like republic. So now, Heaven be praised, Venice is no longer to me a bare and a hollow name, which has so long tormented me, — *me,* the mental enemy of mere verbal sounds.

As the first of the gondoliers came up to the ship (they come in order to convey more quickly to Venice those passengers who are in a hurry), I recollected an old plaything, of which, perhaps, I had not thought for twenty years. My father had a beautiful model of a gondola which he had brought with him [*from Italy*]; he set a great value upon it, and it was considered a great treat, when I was allowed to play with it. The first beaks of tinned iron-plate, the black gondola-gratings, all greeted me like old acquaintances, and I experienced again dear emotions of my childhood which had been long unknown.

I am well lodged at the sign of the *Queen of England,* not far from the square of S. Mark, which is, indeed, the chief advantage of the spot. My windows look upon a narrow canal between lofty houses, a bridge of one arch is immediately below me, and directly opposite is a narrow, bustling alley. Thus am I lodged, and here I shall remain until I have made up my packet for Germany, and until I am satiated with the sight of the city. I can now really enjoy the solitude for which I have longed so ardently, for nowhere does a man feel himself more solitary than in a crowd, where he must push his way unknown to every one. . . .

Oct. 6.

This evening I bespoke the celebrated *song* of the mariners, who chaunt Tasso and Ariosto to melodies of their own. This must actually be ordered, as it is not to be heard as a thing, of course, but rather belongs to the half forgotten traditions of former times. I entered a gondola by moon-light, with one *singer* before and the other behind me. They *sing* their *song,* taking up the verses alternately. The melody, which we know through Rousseau, is of a middle kind, between choral and recitative, maintaining throughout the same cadence, with out any fixed time. The modulation is also uniform. . . .

Piazza San Marco

Sitting on the shore of an island, on the bank of a canal, or on the side of a boat, a gondolier will sing away with a loud penetrating voice — the multitude admire force above everything — anxious only to be heard as far as possible. Over the silent mirror it travels far. Another in the distance, who is acquainted with the melody and knows the words, takes it up, and answers with the next verse, and then the first replies, so that the one is as it were the echo of the other. The song continues through whole nights and is kept up without fatigue. The further the singers are from each other, the more touching sounds the strain. The best place for the listener is halfway between the two.

In order to let me hear it, they landed on the bank of the Guidecca, and took up different positions by the canal. I walked backwards and forwards between them, so as to leave the one whose turn it was to sing, and to join the one who had just left off. Then it was that the effect of the strain first opened upon me. As a voice from the distance it sounds in the highest degree strange — as a lament without sadness: it has an incredible effect and is moving even to tears. . . . [The boatman] wished that I could hear the women of the Lido, especially those of Malamocco, and Pelestrina. These also, he told me, chaunted Tasso and Ariosto to the same or similar melodies. He went on: "in the evening, while their husbands are on the sea fishing, they are accustomed to sit on the beach, and with shrill-penetrating voice to make these strains resound, until they catch from the distance the voices of their partners, and in this way they keep up a communication with them." Is not that beautiful? and yet, it is very possible that one who heard them close by, would take little pleasure in such tones which have to vie with the waves of the sea. Human, however, and true becomes the song in this way: thus is life given to the melody, on whose dead elements we should otherwise have been sadly puzzled. It is the song of one solitary, singing at a distance, in the hope that another of kindred feelings and sentiments may hear and answer.

JOHANN WOLFGANG VON GOETHE
Travels in Italy, 1786–88

The songs of the gondoliers, which had so enthralled Goethe, harmonized even more fruitfully with the talents of another German, Richard Wagner. The controversial composer, whose operas exemplify Romanticism in music, settled in Venice in 1858 and died there twenty-five years later.

I began by looking for a residence that would suit me for my prolonged stay. I heard that one of the three Giustiniani palaces, situated not far from the Palazzo Foscari, was at present very little patronised by visitors, on account of its situation, which in the winter is somewhat unfavourable. I found some very spacious and imposing apartments there, all of which they told me would remain uninhabited. I here engaged a large stately room with a spacious bedroom adjoining. I had my luggage quickly transferred there, and on the evening of 30th August I said to myself, 'At last I am living in Venice.' My leading idea was that I could work here undisturbed. I immediately wrote to Zürich asking for my Erard 'Grand' and my bed to be sent on to me, as, with regard to the latter, I felt that I should find out what cold meant in Venice. In addition to this, the grey-washed walls of my large room soon annoyed me, as they were so little suited to the ceiling, which was covered with a fresco which I thought was rather tasteful. I decided to have the walls of the large room covered with hangings of a dark-red shade, even if they were of quite common quality. This immediately caused much trouble; but it seemed to me that it was well worth surmounting, when I gazed down from my balcony with growing satisfaction on the wonderful canal, and said to myself that here I would complete *Tristan*....

. . . I worked till two o'clock, then I got into the gondola that was always in waiting, and was taken along the solemn Grand Canal to the bright Piazzetta, the peculiar charm of which always had a cheerful effect on me. After this I made for my restaurant in the Piazza San Marco, and when I had finished my meal I walked . . . along the Riva. . . .

. . . During one sleepless night, when I felt impelled to go out on to my balcony in the small hours, I heard for the first time the famous old folk-song of the *gondolieri*. I seemed to hear the first call, in the stillness of the night, proceeding from the Rialto about a mile away like a rough lament, and answered in the same tone from a yet further distance in another direction. This melancholy dialogue, which was repeated at longer intervals, affected me so much that I could not fix the very simple musical component parts in my memory. However, on a subsequent occasion I was told that this folk-song was of great poetic interest. As I was returning home late one night on the gloomy canal, the moon appeared suddenly and illuminated the marvellous palaces and the tall figure of my gondolier towering above the stern of the gondola, slowly moving his huge sweep. Suddenly he uttered a deep wail, not unlike the cry of an animal; the cry gradually gained in strength, and formed itself, after a long-drawn 'Oh!' into the simple musical exclamation 'Venezia!' This was followed by other sounds of which I have no distinct recollection, as I was so much moved at the time. Such were the impressions that to me appeared the most characteristic of Venice during my stay there, and they remained with me until the completion of the second act of *Tristan,* and possibly even suggested to me the long-drawn wail of the shepherd's horn at the beginning of the third act.

RICHARD WAGNER
My Life, 1859

MIDNIGHT ADVENTURES

Giovanni Casanova, whose name has become a synonym for debauchery, was born in Venice in 1725, but not until the mid-twentieth century were his frank and scandalous memoirs published in an unabridged version. Arrested for sorcery and witchcraft at the age of thirty, the amorous adventurer experienced a fearsome and far from romantic aspect of life in his native city.

The captain of the men-at-arms came to tell me that he was under orders to take me under *The Leads.* Without a word I followed him. We went by gondola, and after a thousand turnings among the small canals we got into the *Grand Canal,* and landed at the prison quay. After climbing several flights of stairs we crossed a closed bridge which forms the communication between the prisons and the *Doge's* palace, crossing the canal called *Rio di Palazzo.* On the other side of this bridge there is a gallery which we traversed. . . .

. . . I found myself in a dirty garret, thirty-six feet long by twelve broad, badly lighted by a window high up in the roof. I thought this garret was my prison, but I was mistaken; for, taking an enormous key, the gaoler opened a thick door lined with iron, three and a half feet high. . . .

Masked Venetians at a carnival

To make the reader understand how I managed to escape from a place like *The Leads,* I must explain the nature of the locality.

The Leads, used for the confinement of state prisoners, are in fact the lofts of the ducal palace, and take their name from the large plates of lead with which the roof is covered. One can reach them only through the gates of the palace, the prison buildings, or by the bridge of which I have spoken, called the *Bridge of Sighs.* It is impossible to reach the cells without passing through the hall where the *State Inquisitors* hold their meetings, and their secretary has the sole charge of the key, which he gives to the gaoler only for a short time in the early morning whilst he is attending to the prisoners. This is done at daybreak, because otherwise the guards as they came and went would be in the way of those who have to do with the *Council of Ten.* . . .

The prisons are under the roof on two sides of the palace, three to the west (mine being among the number) and four to the east. On the west the roof looks into the court of the palace, and on the east straight on to the canal called *Rio di Palazzo.* On this side the cells are well lighted, and one can stand up straight, which is not the case in the prison where I was, which was distinguished by the name of *Trave,* on account of the enormous beam which deprived me of light. The floor of my cell was directly over the ceiling of the *Inquisitors'* hall, where they commonly met only at night after the sitting of the *Council of Ten,* of which all three are members.

As I knew my ground and the habits of the *Inquisitors* perfectly well, the only way to escape — the only way, at least, which I deemed likely to succeed — was to make a hole in the floor of my cell; but to do this tools must be obtained — a difficult task in a place where all communication with the outside world was forbidden, where neither letters nor visits were allowed. To bribe a guard, a good deal of money would be necessary, and I had none. And supposing that the gaoler and his two guards allowed themselves to be strangled — for my hands were my only weapons — there was always a third guard on duty at the door of the passage, which he locked, and would not open till his fellow who wished to pass through gave him the password. In spite of all these difficulties my only thought was how to escape.

GIOVANNI CASANOVA
Memoirs, 1755

England's most popular novelist, Charles Dickens, created a score of uniquely unforgettable characters — among them Oliver Twist, David Copperfield, Pip, Ebenezer Scrooge, and Madame Defarge. Dickens's sense of outrage at the cruel inequities of the nineteenth century, which formed the seedbed of his fiction, is mirrored in his phantom cruise through Venice.

The glory of the day that broke upon me in this Dream; its freshness, motion, buoyancy; its sparkles of the sun in water; its clear blue sky and rustling air; no waking words can tell. But, from my window, I looked down on boats and barks; on masts, sails, cordage, flags; on groups of busy sailors, working at the cargoes of these vessels; on wide quays, strewn with bales, casks, merchandise of many kinds; on great ships, lying near at hand in stately indolence; on islands, crowned with gorgeous domes and turrets; and where golden crosses glittered in the light, atop of wondrous churches springing from the sea! Going down upon the margin of the green sea, rolling on before the door, and filling all the streets, I came upon a place of such surpassing beauty, and such grandeur, that all the rest was poor and faded in comparison. . . .

I dreamed that I was led on, then, into some jealous rooms, communicating with a prison near the palace; separated from it by a lofty bridge crossing a narrow street; and called, I dreamed, The Bridge of Sighs. . . .

. . . torch in hand, I descended from the cheerful day into two ranges, one below another, of dismal, awful, horrible stone cells. They were quite dark. Each had a loop-hole in its massive wall, where, in the old time, every day, a torch was placed — I dreamed — to light the prisoner within, for half an hour. The captives, by the glimmering of these brief rays, had scratched and cut inscriptions in the blackened vaults. . . .

One cell, I saw, in which no man remained for more than four-and-twenty hours; being marked for dead before he entered it. Hard by, another, and a dismal one, whereto, at midnight, the confessor came — a monk brown-robed, and hooded — gastly in the day, and free bright air, but in the midnight of that murky prison, Hope's extinguisher, and Murder's herald. I had my foot upon the spot, where, at the same dread hour, the shriven prisoner was strangled; and struck my hand upon the guilty door — low browed and stealthy — through which the lumpish sack was carried out into a boat, and rowed away, and drowned where it was death to cast a net. . . .

. . . taking to my boat again, I rode off to a kind of garden or public walk in the sea where there were grass and trees. . . . I stood upon its farthest brink — I stood there, in my dream — and looked, along the ripple, to the setting sun; before me, in the sky and on the deep, a crimson flush; and behind me the whole city resolving into streaks of red and purple, on the water. . . .

But, close about the quays and churches, palaces and prisons: sucking at their walls, and welling up into the secret places of the town: crept the water always. Noiseless and watchful: coiled round and round it, in its many folds, like an old serpent: waiting for the time, I thought, when people should look down into its depths for any stone of the old city that had claimed to be its mistress.

Thus it floated me away, until I awoke in the old marketplace at Verona. I have, many and many a time, thought since, of this strange Dream upon the water: half-wondering if it lie there yet, and if its name be Venice.

CHARLES DICKENS
Pictures from Italy, 1844

Another nineteenth-century novelist, the Frenchman Théophile Gautier, also responded to the gloomy mystery of Venice at night.

To arrive by night in a city of which one has dreamed for long years is a very simple accident of travel, but one which seemed calculated to excite curiosity to the highest degree of exasperation. To enter the abode of one's fancy with bandaged eyes is the most irritating thing in the world. . . .

Our barque first followed a very wide canal, on the border of which were confusedly delineated obscure edifices punctured by a few lighted windows and a few lanterns which turned straggling beams upon the black and quivering water; then it traversed narrow lanes of water, very complicated in their turnings, or at least they seemed so on account of our ignorance of the road.

The storm, which was drawing to a close, still illumined the sky with livid lightnings which betrayed to us deep perspectives and weird embrasures of unknown palaces. Every minute we passed under bridges, both ends of which corresponded with luminous gashes in the compact and sombre mass of the houses. At every turn a night-lamp flickered before a Madonna. . . .

At the top of the arches human forms vaguely watched us pass by, like the gloomy figures of a dream. Sometimes all the lights were extinguished and we advanced in sinister fashion between four species of gloom, — the oily gloom, damp and deep, of the water; the tempestuous gloom of the nocturnal sky; and the opaque gloom of the two walls, on one of which the lantern of our bark caused a reddish reflection which revealed vanishing pedestals, shafts of columns, porticoes, and bars.

All objects in this obscurity touched by any wandering ray assumed appearances which were mysterious, fantastic, weird, and out of proportion. The water, always so formidable at night, added to the effect by its dull lapping, and its unresting life. The light of infrequent street-lamps extended in bloody trails, and the dark waves, black as those of Cocytus, seemed to spread their complaisant mantle over many a crime. We were surprised not to hear some body fall down from a balcony or from a half-opened door.

. . . The old stories of the Three Inquisitors, of the Council of Ten, of the Bridge of Sighs, of the masked spies, of the pitfalls and sink-holes, of the executions at the Canal Orfano — all the melodrama and romantic environment of ancient Venice returned to our memory in spite of ourselves. . . . A cold horror, damp and dark as all that surrounded us, took possession of us and we thought involuntarily of the tirade of Malipiero to Thisbe, when he depicts the fear with which Venice inspires him. This impression, which perhaps may seem exaggerated, is, however, the exact truth, and we think it would be difficult for even the most positive Philistine to avoid. We will go further and maintain that it is the true idea of Venice, the city which seems to have been established by some theatrical decorator, and for which a dramatic author seems to have arranged the customs for the greater interest of the plots and their denouements. The evening shadows restore the mystery which the day lays bare, replace the antique mask and domino upon the citizens, and give to the most simple movements of life the charm of intrigue or of crime. Each door which half opens has the air of permitting a lover or a bravo to pass. Each gondola which glides silently by seems to carry a pair of lovers or a corpse with a stiletto in its heart.

THÉOPHILE GAUTIER
Journeys in Italy, 1852

Teatro la Fenice

ALONG THE GRAND CANAL

The floating fantasy that is Venice has appeared in countless literary works, including several by the American novelist Henry James. In The Aspern Papers, *an American schemes to obtain the letters of Jeffrey Aspern from that dead poet's elderly mistress – and becomes involved in a reluctant courtship of her faded niece.*

We swept in the course of five minutes into the Grand Canal; whereupon she uttered a murmur of ecstasy as fresh as if she had been a tourist just arrived. She had forgotten the splendour of the great water-way on a clear summer evening, and how the sense of floating between marble palaces and reflected lights disposed the mind to freedom and ease. We floated long and far, and though my friend gave no high-pitched voice to her glee I was sure of her full surrender. She was more than pleased, she was transported; the whole thing was an immense liberation. The gondola moved with slow strokes, to give her time to enjoy it, and she listened to the plash of the oars, which grew louder and more musically liquid as we passed into narrow canals, as if it were a revelation of Venice. When I asked her how long it was since she had thus floated she answered: "Oh I don't know; a long time – not since my aunt began to be ill." This was not the only show of her extreme vagueness about the previous years and the line marking off the period of Miss Bordereau's eminence. I was not at liberty to keep her out long, but we took a considerable *giro* before going to the Piazza. I asked her no questions, holding off by design from her life at home and the things I wanted to know; I poured, rather, treasures of information about the objects before and around us into her ears, describing also Florence and Rome, discoursing on the charms and advantages of travel. She reclined, receptive, on the deep leather cushions, turned her eyes conscientiously to everything I noted and never mentioned to me till some time afterwards that she might be supposed to know Florence better than I, as she had lived there for years with her kinswoman. At last she said with the shy impatience of a child: "Are we not really going to the Piazza? That's what I want to see!" I immediately gave the order that we should go straight. . . .

. . . the gondola approached the Piazzetta. After we had disembarked I asked my companion if she would rather walk round the square or go and sit before the great café; to which she replied that she would do whichever I liked best – I must only remember again how little time she had. I assured her there was plenty to do both, and we made the circuit of the long arcades. Her spirits revived at the sight of the bright shop-windows, and she lingered and stopped, admiring or disapproving of their contents, asking me what I thought of things, theorising about prices. . . . We sat down at last in the crowded circle at Florian's, finding an unoccupied table among those that were ranged in the square. It was a splendid night and all the world out-of-doors; Miss Tina couldn't have wished the elements more auspicious for her return to society. I saw she felt it all even more than she told, but her impressions were well-nigh too many for her. She had forgotten the attraction of the world and was learning that she had for the best years of her life been rather mercilessly cheated of it. This didn't make her angry; but as she took in the charming scene her face had, in spite of its smile of appreciation, the flush of a wounded surprise. She didn't speak, sunk in the sense of opportunities, for ever lost, that ought to have been easy.

HENRY JAMES
The Aspern Papers, 1888

The Flame of Life *by Gabriele D'Annunzio, based on the Italian novelist's liaison with Eleonora Duse — whose fame as an actress was rivaled only by that of Sarah Bernhardt — caused an international scandal when it was published in 1900.*

A sound of applause burst from the Passage of San Gregorio, echoing along the Grand Canal, re-echoing in the precious discs of porphyry and serpentine adorning the house of the Darios, that stooped under their weight like a decrepit courtesan under the pomp of her jewels.

The royal barge was passing. . . .

The two occupants of the gondola saluted the barge as it passed them. The Queen, blonde, rosy, illuminated by the freshness of the inexhaustible smile that was for ever rippling among the pale meshes of her Buranese laces, looked back, moved by an impulse of spontaneous curiosity, as she recognized the poet of *Persephone* and the great tragic actress. By her side was Andriana Duodo, the patroness of Burano, the industrious little island where she cultivated a dainty garden of thread for the marvellous renewing of antique flowers.

"Don't you think, Stelio, that those two women have twin smiles?" La Foscarina said, watching the water gurgle in the furrow left by the receding gondola, where the reflection of that double glamour seemed to prolong itself. . . .

A fresh clamour, louder and longer, rose from between the two watchful columns of granite, as the barge came to shore by the crowded Piazzetta. A confused roar, like the imaginary rushing that animates the spirals of some sea-shells, filled the open spaces of the ducal balconies at the surging of the dense, dark multitude. Then, suddenly, the shout rose higher in the limpid air, breaking up against the slim forest of the marbles, vaulting over the brow of the taller statues, shooting beyond the pinnacles and the crosses, dispersing in the far distances of twilight. The manifold harmonies of the sacred and pagan architectures all over which the Ionic modulations of the Biblioteca ran like an agile melody, continued unbroken in the pause which again followed, and the summit of the naked tower rose like a mystic cry. And that silent music of motionless lines was so powerful, in its contrast with the spectacle of an anxious multitude, that it created almost visibly the phantom of some richer and more beautiful life. That multitude, too, seemed to feel the divinity of the hour, and in the greeting it sent up to the modern symbol of royalty stepping on its ancient landing-place, the fair Queen beaming with her inextinguishable smile, perhaps it exhaled its obscure aspiration to transcend the narrowness of its daily life and to reap the harvest of eternal poetry growing over its stones and its waters. In those men, oppressed by the tedium and labour of their long mediocrity, the strong covetous souls of their forefathers, who had applauded so many returning conquerors of the sea, seemed to be waking up confusedly, and as they woke they seemed to remember the rush of the air, stirred by the hissing, implacable banners of old that had shamed enemies without number as they dropped to rest, refolding like the great wings of victory.

"Do you know, Perdita," suddenly asked Stelio,— "do you know of any other place in the world like Venice, in its power of stimulating at certain moments all the power of human life, and of exciting every desire to the point of fever? Do you know of any more terrible temptress?"

GABRIELE D'ANNUNZIO
The Flame of Life, 1900

St. Mark's basin

In Thomas Mann's haunting novella, Death in Venice, *the city itself becomes a character within the story. Considered by many literary critics to be the foremost German author of the twentieth century, Mann was awarded the Nobel Prize for literature in 1929.*

He spent two hours in his room [at the Hotel Excelsior on the Lido], and in the afternoon he rode in the *vaporetto* across the foul-smelling lagoon to Venice. He got off at San Marco, took tea on the Piazza, and then, in accord with his schedule for the day, he went for a walk through the streets. Yet it was this walk which produced a complete reversal in his attitudes and his plans.

An offensive sultriness lay over the streets. The air was so heavy that the smells pouring out of homes, stores, and eating-houses became mixed with oil, vapours, clouds of perfumes, and still other odours – and these would not blow away, but hung in layers. Cigarette smoke remained suspended, disappearing very slowly. The crush of people along the narrow streets irritated rather than entertained the walker. The farther he went, the more he was depressed by the repulsive condition resulting from the combination of sea air and sirocco, which was at the same time both stimulating and enervating. He broke into an uncomfortable sweat. His eyes failed him, his chest became tight, he had a fever, the blood was pounding in his head. He fled from the crowded business streets across a bridge into the walks of the poor. On a quiet square, one of those forgotten and enchanting places which lie in the interior of Venice, he rested at the brink of a well, dried his forehead, and realized that he would have to leave here.

For the second and last time it had been demonstrated that this city in this kind of weather was decidedly unhealthy for him. It seemed foolish to attempt a stubborn resistance, while the prospects for a change of wind were completely uncertain. A quick decision was called for. It was not possible to go home this soon. Neither summer nor winter quarters were prepared to receive him. But this was not the only place where there were sea and beach; and elsewhere these could be found without the lagoon and its malarial mists. He remembered a little watering-place not far from Trieste which had been praised to him. Why not there? And without delay. . . .

When he had returned to the hotel, he announced at the office before dinner that unforeseen developments necessitated his departure the following morning. He was assured of their regrets. He settled his accounts. He dined, and spent the warm evening reading the newspapers in a rocking-chair on the rear terrace. Before going to bed he got his luggage all ready for departure. . . .

. . . he left, distributed tips, was ushered out by the small gentle manager in the French frock-coat, and made off from the hotel on foot, as he had come, going along the white blossoming avenue which crossed the island to the steamer bridge, accompanied by the house servant carrying his hand luggage. He arrived, took his place – and then followed a painful journey through all the depths of regret.

It was the familiar trip across the lagoon, past San Marco, up the Grand Canal. Aschenbach sat on the circular bench at the bow, his arm supported against the railing, shading his eyes with his hand. The public gardens were left behind, the Piazzetta opened up once more in princely splendour and was gone, then came the great flock of palaces, and as the channel made a turn the magnificently slung marble arch of the Rialto came into view. The traveller was watching; his emotions were in conflict. The atmosphere of the city, this slightly foul smell of sea and swamp which he had been so anxious to avoid — he breathed it now in deep, exquisitely painful draughts. Was it possible that he had not known, had not considered, just how much he was attached to all this? What had been a partial misgiving this morning, a faint doubt as to the advisability of his move, now became a distress, a positive misery, a spiritual hunger, and so bitter that it frequently brought tears to his eyes, while he told himself that he could not possibly have foreseen it. Hardest of all to bear, at times completely insufferable, was the thought that he would never see Venice again, that this was a leave-taking for ever. Since it had been shown for the second time that the city affected his health, since he was compelled for the second time to get away in all haste, from now on he would have to consider it a place impossible and forbidden to him, a place which he was not equal to, and which it would be foolish for him to visit again. Yes, he felt that if he left now, he would be shamefaced and defiant enough never to see again the beloved city which had twice caused him a physical break-down. And of a sudden this struggle between his desires and his physical strength seemed to the aging man so grave and important, his physical defeat seemed so dishonourable, so much a challenge to hold out at any cost, that he could not understand the ready submissiveness of the day before, when he had decided to give in without attempting any serious resistance.

The burning of San Marcuola Church

Meanwhile the steamboat was nearing the station; pain and perplexity increased, he became distracted. In his affliction, he felt that it was impossible to leave, and just as impossible to turn back. The conflict was intense as he entered the station. It was very late; there was not a moment to lose if he was to catch the train. He wanted to, and he did not want to. But time was pressing; it drove him on. He hurried to get his ticket, and looked about in the tumult of the hall for the officer on duty here from the hotel. The man appeared and announced that the large trunk had been transferred. Transferred already? Yes, thank you — to Como. To Como? And in the midst of hasty running back and forth, angry questions and confused answers, it came to light that the trunk had already been sent with other foreign baggage from the express office of the Hotel Excelsior in a completely wrong direction.

Aschenbach had difficulty in preserving the expression which was required under these circumstances. He was almost convulsed with an adventurous delight, an unbelievable hilarity. The employee rushed off to see if it were still possible to stop the trunk, and, as was to be expected, he returned with nothing accomplished. Aschenbach declared that he did not want to travel without his trunk, but had decided to go back and wait at the beach hotel for its return. Was the company's motorboat still at the station? The man assured him that it was lying at the door. With Italian volubility he persuaded the clerk at the ticket window to redeem the cancelled ticket, he swore that they would act speedily, that no time or money would be spared in recovering the trunk promptly, and — so the strange thing happened that, twenty minutes after his arrival at the station, the traveller found himself again on the Grand Canal, returning to the Lido.

THOMAS MANN
Death in Venice, 1913

Another Nobel Prize winner, the American novelist Ernest Hemingway, also used Venice as the setting for a novel. The narrator of Across the River and Into the Trees *is an aging World War I veteran who returns to the city he helped liberate.*

They were through the dull part of the canal that runs from Piazzale Roma to Ca'Foscari, though none of it is dull, the Colonel thought.

It doesn't all have to be palaces nor churches. Certainly that isn't dull. He looked to the right, the starboard, he thought. I'm on the water. It was a long low pleasant building and there was a trattoria next to it.

I ought to live here. On retirement pay I could make it all right. No Gritti Palace. A room in a house like that and the tides and the boats going by. I could read in the mornings and walk around town before lunch and go every day to see the Tintorettos at the Accademia and to the Scuola San Rocco and eat in good cheap joints behind the market, or, maybe, the woman that ran the house would cook in the evenings.

I think it would be better to have lunch out and get some exercise walking. It's a good town to walk in. I guess the best, probably. I never walked in it that it wasn't fun. I could learn it really well, he thought, and then I'd have that. . . .

And all this time he had been watching the bow of the beat-up beautifully varnished, delicately brass-striped boat, with the brass all beautifully polished, cut the brown water, and seen the small traffic problems.

They went under the white bridge and under the unfinished wood bridge. Then they left the red bridge on the right and passed under the first high-flying white bridge. Then there was the black iron fret-work bridge on the canal leading into the Rio Nuovo and they passed the two stakes chained together but not touching: like us the Colonel thought. He watched the tide pull at them and he saw how the chains had worn the wood since he first had seen them. That's us, he thought. That's our monument. And how many monuments are there to us in the canals of this town?

Then they still went slowly until the great lantern that was on the right of the entrance to the Grand Canal where the engine commenced its metallic agony that produced a slight increase in speed. . . .

They were moving up the Grand Canal now and it was easy to see where your friends lived.

"That's the house of the Contessa Dandolo," the Colonel said. . . .

Her *palazzo* was pleasant looking, set well back from the Canal with a garden in front and a landing place of its own where many gondolas had come, in their various times, bringing hearty, cheerful, sad and disillusioned people. But most of them had been cheerful because they were going to see the Contessa Dandolo.

Now, beating up the Canal, against the cold wind off the mountains, and with the houses as clear and sharp as on a winter day, which, of course, it was, they saw the old magic of the city and its beauty. But it was conditioned, for the Colonel, by his knowing many of the people who lived in the palazzos; or if no one lived there now, knowing to what use the different places had been put.

There's Alvarito's mother's house, he thought, and did not say.

She never lives there much and stays out in the country house near Treviso where they have trees. She's tired of there not being trees in Venice. She lost a fine man and nothing really interests her now except efficiency.

But the family at one time lent the house to George Gordon, Lord Byron, and nobody sleeps now in Byron's bed nor in the other bed, two flights below, where he used to sleep with the gondolier's wife. They are not sacred, nor relics. They are just extra beds that were not used afterwards for various reasons, or possibly to respect Lord Byron who was well loved in this town, in spite of all the errors he committed. You have to be a tough boy in this town to be loved, the Colonel thought. They never cared anything for Robert Browning, nor Mrs. Robert Browning, nor for their dog. They weren't Venetians no matter how well he wrote of it. And what is a tough boy, he asked himself. You use it so loosely you should be able to define it. I suppose it is a man who will make his play and then backs it up. Or just a man who backs his play. And I'm not thinking of the theatre, he thought. Lovely as the theatre can be.

ERNEST HEMINGWAY
Across the River and Into the Trees, 1950

THE BEAUTY OF THIS THY VENICE

Percy Bysshe Shelley was among the many prominent poets inspired by Venice. During his stay at Lord Byron's villa in the nearby town of Este in 1818, the Englishman composed Lines Written Among the Euganean Hills.

Beneath is spread like a green sea
The waveless plain of Lombardy,
Bounded by the vaporous air,
Islanded by cities fair.
Underneath day's azure eyes,
Ocean's nursling, Venice lies,
A peopled labyrinth of walls,
Amphitrite's destined halls,
Which her hoary sire now paves
With his blue and beaming waves.
Lo! the sun upsprings behind,
Broad, red, radiant, half-reclined
On the level quivering line
Of the waters crystalline;
And before that chasm of light,
As within a furnace bright,
Column, tower, and dome and spire
Shine like obelisks of fire,
Pointing with inconstant motion
From the altar of dark ocean
To the sapphire-tinted skies;
As the flames of sacrifice
From the marble shrines did rise
As to pierce the dome of gold
Where Apollo spoke of old.

Sun-girt City! thou hast been
Ocean's child, and then his queen;
Now is come a darker day.
And thou soon must be his prey,

Skating on the frozen lagoon

If the power that raised thee here
Hallow so thy watery bier.
A less drear ruin then than now,
With thy conquest-branded brow
Stooping to the slave of slaves
From thy throne among the waves,
Wilt thou be, when the sea-mew
Flies, as once before it flew,
O'er thine isles depopulate,
And all is in its ancient state,
Save where many a palace-gate
With green sea-flowers overgrown
Like a rock of ocean's own,
Topples o'er the abandoned sea
As the tides change sullenly.
The fisher on his watery way,
Wandering at the close of day,
Will spread his sail and seize his oar
Till he pass the gloomy shore,
Lest thy dead should, from their sleep
Bursting o'er the starlight deep,
Lead a rapid masque of death
O'er the waters of his path.

PERCY BYSSHE SHELLEY
Lines Written Among the Euganean Hills, 1819

The controversial and eccentric American poet Ezra Pound lived in self-imposed exile in Venice from 1958 until his death in 1972. Pound's second volume of verse, published in 1909, included a tribute to the city that later became his home.

O Dieu, purifiez nos coeurs!
Purifiez nos coeurs!

Yea, the lines hast thou laid unto me
in pleasant places,
And the beauty of this thy Venice
has thou shown unto me
Until is its loveliness become unto me
a thing of tears.

O God, what great kindness
have we done in times past
and forgotten it;
That thou givest this wonder unto us,
O God of waters? . . .

Yea, the glory of the shadow
of thy Beauty hath walked
Upon the shadow of the waters

In this thy Venice.
And before the holiness
Of the shadow of thy handmaid
Have I hidden mine eyes,
O God of waters.

O God of silence
Purifiez nos coeurs,
Purifiez nos coeurs,
O God of waters,
make clean our hearts within us
And our lips to show forth thy praise.
For I have seen the
Shadow of this thy Venice
Floating upon the waters,
And thy stars

Have seen this thing out of their far courses
Have they seen this thing,
O God of waters.
Even as are thy stars
Silent unto us in their far-coursing,
Even so is mine heart
become silent within me.

EZRA POUND
Night Litany, 1908

DISSENTING VOICES

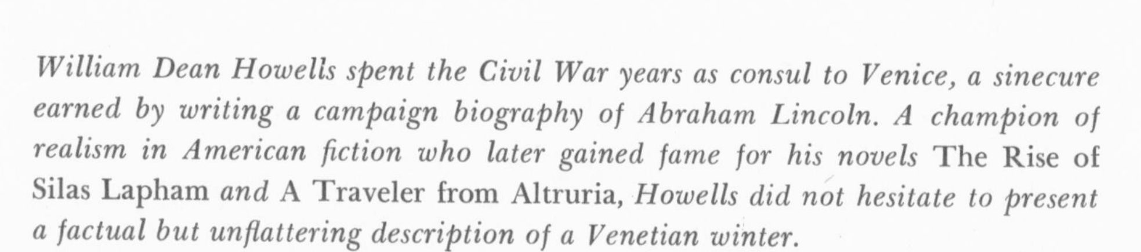

William Dean Howells spent the Civil War years as consul to Venice, a sinecure earned by writing a campaign biography of Abraham Lincoln. A champion of realism in American fiction who later gained fame for his novels The Rise of Silas Lapham *and* A Traveler from Altruria, *Howells did not hesitate to present a factual but unflattering description of a Venetian winter.*

It was winter . . . when I first came to Venice, and my experiences of the city were not all purely aesthetic. There was, indeed, an every-day roughness and discomfort in the weather, which travellers passing their first winter in Italy find it hard to reconcile with the habitual ideas of the season's clemency in the South. . . .

The Germans have introduced stoves at Venice, but they are not in much favor with the Italians, who think their heat unwholesome, and endure a degree of cold, in their wish to dispense with fire, which we of the winterlands know nothing of in our houses. They pay for their absurd prejudice with terrible chilblains; and their hands, which suffer equally with their feet, are, in the case of those most exposed to the cold, objects pitiable and revolting to behold when the itching and the effort to allay it has turned them into bloated masses of sores. It is not a pleasant thing to speak of; and the constant sight of the affliction among people who bring you bread, cut you cheese, and weigh you out sugar by no means reconciles the Northern stomach to its prevalence. . . .

The houses are, naturally enough in this climate, where there are eight

An elaborate ceremonial barge

months of summer in the year, all built with a view to coolness in summer, and the rooms which are not upon the ground-floor are very large, lofty, and cold. In the palaces, indeed, there are two suites of apartments, — the smaller and cozier suite upon the first floor for the winter, and the grander and airier chambers and saloons above, for defence against the insidious heats of the sirocco. But, for the most part, people must occupy the same room summer and winter, the sole change being in the strip of carpet laid meagrely before the sofa during the latter season. In the comparatively few houses where carpets are the rule, and not the exception, they are always removed during the summer, — for the triple purpose of sparing them some months' wear, banishing fleas and other domestic insects, and showing off the beauty of the oiled and shining pavement, which in the meanest of houses is tasteful, and in many of the better sort is often inwrought with figures and designs of mosaic work. All the floors in Venice are of stone; and whether of marble flags, or of that species of composition formed of dark cement, with fragments of colored marble imbedded, and smoothed and polished to the most glassy and even surface, and the general effect and complexion of petrified plum-pudding, all the floors are death-cold in winter. People sit with their feet upon cushions, and their bodies muffled in furs and wadded gowns. When one goes out into the sun, one often finds an overcoat too heavy, but it never gives warmth enough in the house, where the Venetian sometimes wears it. Indeed, the sun is recognized by Venetians as the only legitimate source of heat, and they sell his favor at fabulous prices to such foreigners as take the lodgings into which he shines. . . .

In the winter, the whole city *sniffs,* and if the Pipchin theory of the effect of sniffing upon the eternal interests of the soul be true, few people go to heaven from Venice. I sometimes wildly wondered if Desdemona, in *her* time, sniffed, and found little comfort in the reflection that Shylock must have had a cold in his head. There is comparative warmth in the broad squares before the churches, but the narrow streets are bitter thorough-draughts, and fell influenza lies in wait for its prey in all those picturesque, seducing little courts. . . .

It is, however, in the churches, whose cool twilight and airy height one finds so grateful in summer, that the sharpest malice of the winter is felt; and having visited a score of them soon after my arrival, I deferred the remaining seventy-five or eighty, together with the gallery of the Academy, until advancing spring should in some degree have mitigated the severity of their temperature. As far as my imagination affected me, I thought the Gothic churches much more tolerable than the temples of Renaissance art. The empty bareness of these, with their huge marbles and their soulless splendors of theatrical sculpture, their frescoed roofs and broken arches, was insufferable. The arid grace of Palladio's architecture was especially grievous to the sense in cold weather; and I warn the traveller who goes to see the lovely Madonnas of Bellini to beware how he trusts himself in winter to the gusty, arctic magnificence of the church of the Redentore. But by all means the coldest church in the city is that of the Jesuits, which those who have seen it will remember for its famous marble drapery. This base, mechanical surprise (for it is a trick, and not art) is effected by inlaying the white marble of columns and pulpits and altars with a certain pattern of verd-antique. The workmanship is marvellously skilful and the material costly, but it only gives the church the effect of being draped in damask linen; and even where the marble is carven in vast and heavy folds over a pulpit to simulate a curtain, or wrought in figures on the steps of the high altar to represent a carpet, it has no richness of effect, but a poverty, a coldness, a harshness, indescribably table-clothy. I think all this has tended to chill the soul of the sacristan, who is the feeblest and thinnest sacristan conceivable, with a frost of white hair on his temples quite incapable of thawing. In this dreary sanctuary is one of Titian's great paintings, The Martyrdom of St. Lawrence, to which (though it is so cunningly disposed as to light that no one ever yet saw the whole picture at once) you turn involuntarily, envious of the Saint toasting so comfortably on his gridiron amid all that frigidity.

WILLIAM DEAN HOWELLS
Venetian Life, 1866

The Piazzetta

One purpose of The Innocents Abroad *was "to suggest to the reader how* he *would be likely to see Europe and the East if he looked at them with his own eyes instead of the eyes of those who traveled in those countries before him." True to form, America's genial iconoclast, Samuel Langhorne Clemens — writing under his pseudonym, Mark Twain — took a decided dislike to Venice.*

We reached Venice at eight in the evening, and entered a hearse belonging to the Grand Hotel d'Europe. At any rate, it was more like a hearse than anything else, though, to speak by the card, it was a gondola. And this was the storied gondola of Venice! — the fairy boat in which the princely cavaliers of the olden time were wont to cleave the waters of the moonlit canals and look the eloquence of love into the soft eyes of patrician beauties, while the gay gondolier in silken doublet touched his guitar and sang as only gondoliers can sing! This the famed gondola and this the gorgeous gondolier! — the one an inky, rusty old canoe with a sable hearse-body clapped on to the middle of it, and the other a mangy, barefooted guttersnipe with a portion of his raiment on exhibition which should have been sacred from public scrutiny. . . .

I began to feel that the old Venice of song and story had departed forever. But I was too hasty. In a few minutes we swept gracefully out into the Grand Canal, and under the mellow moonlight the Venice of poetry and romance stood revealed. Right from the water's edge rose long lines of stately palaces of marble; gondolas were gliding swiftly hither and thither and disappearing suddenly through unsuspected gates and alleys; ponderous stone bridges threw their shadows athwart the glittering waves. There was life and motion everywhere, and yet everywhere there was a hush, a stealthy sort of stillness, that was suggestive of secret enterprises of bravoes and of lovers; and, clad half in moonbeams and half in mysterious shadows, the grim old mansions of the Republic seemed to have an expression about them of having an eye out for just such enterprises as these at that same moment. Music came floating over the waters — Venice was complete. . . .

What a funny old city this Queen of the Adriatic is! Narrow streets, vast, gloomy marble palaces, black with the corroding damps of centuries, and all partly submerged; no dry land visible anywhere, and no sidewalks worth mentioning; if you want to go to church, to the theater, or to the restaurant, you must call a gondola. It must be a paradise for cripples, for verily a man has no use for legs here. . . .

. . . We have seen pictures of martyrs enough, and saints enough, to regenerate the world. . . . to me it seemed that when I had seen one of these martyrs I had seen them all. They all have a marked family resemblance to each other, they dress alike, in coarse monkish robes and sandals, they are all bald-headed, they all stand in about the same attitude, and without exception they are gazing heavenward with countenances which the Ainsworths, the Mortons, and the Williamses, *et fils,* inform me are full of "expression". . . .

But humble as we are, and unpretending, in the matter of art, our researches among the painted monks and martyrs have not been wholly in vain. We have striven hard to learn. We have had some success. We have mastered some things, possibly of trifling import in the eyes of the learned, but to us they give pleasure, and we take as much pride in our little acquirements as do others who have learned far more, and we love to display them full as well. When we see a monk going about with a lion and looking tranquilly up to heaven, we know that that is St. Mark. When we see a monk with a book and a pen, looking tranquilly up to heaven, trying to think of a word, we know that that is St. Matthew. When we see a monk sitting on a rock, looking tranquilly up to heaven, with a human skull beside him, and without other baggage, we know that that is St. Jerome. Because we know that he always went flying light in the matter of baggage. When we see a party looking tranquilly up to heaven, unconscious that his body is shot through and through with arrows, we know that that is St. Sebastian. When we see other monks looking tranquilly up to heaven, but have no trademark, we always ask who those parties are. We do this because we humbly wish to learn. We have seen thirteen thousand St. Jeromes, and twenty-two thousand St. Marks, and sixteen thousand St. Matthews, and sixty thousand St. Sebastians, and four millions of assorted monks, undesignated, and we feel encouraged to believe that when we have seen some more of these various pictures, and had a larger experience, we shall begin to take an absorbing interest in them like our cultivated countrymen from *Amerique.*

SAMUEL LANGHORNE CLEMENS
The Innocents Abroad, 1869

Herbert Spencer, the English philosopher and social scientist who was instrumental in popularizing Darwin's theory of evolution, found much to criticize during his visit to Venice in 1880.

The next morning found us at Venice. Here I suppose I ought to have remained some time; but I find by my diary, rather to my surprise, that my stay did not extend beyond three days. Doubtless my impatience to get home was the chief cause of this abridgment; joined, perhaps, with the fact that "the stones of Venice" did not produce in me so much enthusiasm as in many. Not that I failed to derive much pleasure; but the pleasure was less multitudinous in its sources than that which is felt, or is alleged to be felt, by the majority. . . .

. . . In the separate buildings in which architects aimed at beauty they have rarely achieved it; but they have unawares achieved it in the assemblages of buildings. Houses severally placed without reference to effect, present everywhere charming combinations of form and colours; so that, especially in the smaller canals, every turn furnishes a picture.

Astonished at these heretical opinions, the reader will doubtless ask for justifications, and I cannot well avoid giving them. Speaking generally, then, say of the palaces along the Grand Canal, my first criticism is that they are fundamentally defective in presenting to the eye nothing more than decorated flat surfaces. No fine architectural effect can be had without those advancing and retreating masses which produce broad contrasts of light and shade and yield variety in the perspective lines. This is not all. A flat *façade* has not only the defects that its perspective lines are monotonous and its contrasts of light and shade insufficient; but it has, in too conspicuous a way, the aspect of artificiality. Its decorative elements – columns placed against the surface, pilasters stuck upon it, reveals cut into it, string-courses running along it, *plaques* or medallions or carved wreaths attached in plain spaces – are all obviously designed for effect. They form no needful parts of the structure, but are merely superposed; and clearly tell the spectator that they are there simply to be admired. But any work of art is faulty if it suggests an eager desire for admiration in the artist – if it suggests that neither the thought of use nor the simple perception of beauty moved him, but that he was chiefly moved by love of applause. It is a recognized truth that that is the highest art which hides the art, and an ornamented flat surface necessarily fails in this respect; since it discloses unmistakably the fact that almost everything done to the surface is done for the sake of appearance. As illustrations of my meaning I may name the Dario, the Corner-Spinelli, and the Rezzonico palaces. The best of these flat *façades* is that of the Scuola di San Rocco . . . because the decorative element . . . is less obtrusive. . . .

Rialto Bridge and the Grand Canal

And what about St. Mark's? Well, I admit that it is a fine sample of barbaric architecture. I used the word barbaric advisedly; for it has the trait distinctive of semi-civilized art – excess of decoration. This trait is seen in an Egyptian temple, with its walls and columns covered with coloured frescoes and hieroglyphs. It is seen in oriental dresses, of which the fabric is almost hidden by gold braiding and crusts of jewellery. It is seen in such articles of Indian manufacture as cabinets and boxes, having surfaces filled with fret-works of carving. And in medieval days throughout Europe, it was habitually displayed on articles belonging to those of rank – pieces of furniture profusely inlaid; suits of armour covered everywhere with elaborate chasing; swords, guns, and pistols, with blades, barrels and stocks chased and carved from one end to the other. The characteristic of barbaric art is that it leaves no space without ornament; and this is the characteristic of St. Mark's. The spandrils of the lower tier of arches are the only parts of the *façade* not crammed with decorative work. This is an error which more developed art avoids. Practically, if not theoretically, it recognizes the fact that, to obtain the contrasts requisite for good effect, there must be large areas which are relatively plain, to serve as foils to the enriched areas. A work of art which is full of small contrasts and without any great contrasts, sins against the fundamental principles of beauty; and a contrast above all others indispensable is that between simplicity and complexity.

Archeologically considered, St. Mark's is undoubtedly precious; but it is not precious aesthetically considered. Unfortunately many people confound the two.

HERBERT SPENCER
An Autobiography, 1904

Sympathetic to those who could not or would not succumb to the charm of Venice, Henry James suggested a simple and effective countermeasure.

It is possible to dislike Venice, and to entertain the sentiment in a responsible and intelligent manner. There are travellers who think the place odious, and those who are not of this opinion often find themselves wishing that the others were only more numerous. The sentimental tourist's sole quarrel with his Venice is that he has too many competitors there. He likes to be alone; to be original; to have (to himself, at least) the air of making discoveries. The Venice of to-day is a vast museum where the little wicket that admits you is perpetually turning and creaking, and you march through the institution with a herd of fellow-gazers. There is nothing left to discover or describe, and originality of attitude is completely impossible. This is often very annoying; you can only turn your back on your impertinent playfellow and curse his want of delicacy. But this is not the fault of Venice; it is the fault of the rest of the world. The fault of Venice is that, though it is easy to admire, it is not so easy to live in it. After you have been there a week and the bloom of novelty has rubbed off, you wonder whether you can accommodate yourself to the peculiar conditions. Your old habits become impracticable, and you find yourself obliged to form new ones of an undesirable and unprofitable character. You are tired of your gondola (or you think you are) and you have seen all the principal pictures and heard the names of the palaces announced a dozen times by your gondolier, who brings them out almost as impressively as if he were an English butler bawling titles into a drawing-room. You have walked several hundred times round the Piazza and bought several bushels of photographs. You have visited the antiquity-mongers whose horrible sign-boards dishonour some of the grandest vistas in the Grand Canal; you have tried the opera and found it very bad; you have bathed at the Lido and found the water flat. You have begun to have a shipboard-feeling – to regard the Piazza as an enormous saloon and the Riva degli Schiavoni as a promenade-deck. You are obstructed and encaged; your desire for space is unsatisfied; you miss your usual exercise. You try to take a walk and you fail, and meantime, as I say, you have come to regard your gondola as a sort of magnified baby's cradle. You have no desire to be rocked to sleep, though you are sufficiently kept awake by the irritation produced, as you gaze across the shallow lagoon, by the attitude of the perpetual gondolier, with his turned-out toes, his protruded chin, his absurdly unscientific stroke. The canals have a horrible smell, and the everlasting Piazza, where you have looked repeatedly at every article in every shop-window and found them all rubbish, where the young Venetians who sell bead bracelets and "panoramas" are perpetually thrusting their wares at you, where the same tightly-buttoned officers are for ever sucking the same black weeds, at the same empty tables, in front of the same cafes – the Piazza, as I say, has resolved itself into a magnificent tread-mill. This is the state of mind of those shallow inquirers who find Venice all very well for a week; and if in such a state of mind you take your departure you act with fatal rashness. The loss is your own, moreover; it is not – with all deference to your personal attractions – that of your companions who remain behind; for though there are some disagreeable things in Venice there is nothing so disagreeable as the visitors. The conditions are peculiar, but your intolerance of them evaporates before it has had time to become a prejudice. When you have called for the bill to go, pay it and remain, and you will find on the morrow that you are deeply attached to Venice. It is by living there from day to day that you feel the fulness of its charm; that you invite its exquisite influence to sink into your spirit. The place is as changeable as a nervous woman, and you know it only when you know all the aspects of its beauty. It has high spirits or low, it is pale or red, grey or pink, cold or warm, fresh or wan, according to the weather or the hour. It is always interesting and almost always sad; but it has a thousand occasional graces and is always liable to happy accidents. You become extraordinarily fond of these things; you count upon them; they make part of your life. Tenderly fond you become; there is something indefinable in those depths of personal acquaintance that gradually establish themselves. The place seems to personify itself, to become human and sentient and conscious of your affection. You desire to embrace it, to caress it, to possess it; and finally a soft sense of possession grows up and your visit becomes a perpetual love-affair.

HENRY JAMES
Portraits of Places, 1883

GOD AND GOLD IN VENICE

The Stones of Venice, *a three-volume work first published in 1851–53 by the English art historian and critic John Ruskin, remains the definitive study of Venice as an esthetic and architectural wonder.*

As we advance slowly, the vast tower of St. Mark seems to lift itself visibly forth from the level field of chequered stones; and, on each side, the countless arches prolong themselves into ranged symmetry, as if the rugged and irregular houses that pressed together above us in the dark alley had been struck back into sudden obedience and lovely order, and all their rude casements and broken walls had been transformed into arches charged with goodly sculpture, and fluted shafts of delicate stone.

And well may they fall back, for beyond those troops of ordered arches there rises a vision out of the earth, and all the great square seems to have opened from it in a kind of awe, that we may see it far away; — a multitude of pillars and white domes, clustered into a long low pyramid of colored light; a treasure-heap, it seems, partly of gold, and partly of opal and mother-of-pearl, hollowed beneath into five great vaulted porches, ceiled with fair mosaic, and beset with sculpture of alabaster, clear as amber and delicate as ivory, — sculpture fantastic and involved, of palm leaves and lilies, and grapes and pomegranates, and birds clinging and fluttering among the branches, all twined together into an endless network of buds and plumes; and, in the midst of it, the solemn forms of angels, sceptred, and robed to the feet, and leaning to each other across the gates, their figures indistinct among the gleaming of the golden ground through the leaves beside them, interrupted and dim, like the morning light as it faded back among the branches of Eden, when first its gates were angel-guarded long ago. And round the walls of the porches . . . a confusion of delight, amidst which the breasts of the Greek horses are seen blazing in their breadth of golden strength, and the St. Mark's Lion, lifted on a blue field covered with stars, until at last, as if in ecstacy, the crests of the arches break into a marble foam, and toss themselves far into the blue sky in flashes and wreaths of sculptured spray, as if the breakers on the Lido shore had been frost-bound before they

The Bucentaur

fell, and the sea-nymphs had inlaid them with coral and amethyst. . . .

And what effect has this splendor on those who pass beneath it? You may walk from sunrise to sunset, to and fro, before the gateway of St. Mark's, and you will not see an eye lifted to it, nor a countenance brightened by it. Priest and layman, soldier and civilian, rich and poor, pass by it alike regardlessly. Up to the very recesses of the porches, the meanest tradesmen of the city push their counters; nay, the foundations of its pillars are themselves the seats — not "of them that sell doves" for sacrifice, but of the vendors of toys and caricatures. Round the whole square in front of the church there is almost a continuous line of cafés, where the idle Venetians of the middle classes lounge, and read empty journals; in its centre the Austrian bands play during the time of vespers, their martial music jarring with the organ notes, — the march drowning the miserere, and the sullen crowd thickening round them, — a crowd, which, if it had its will, would stiletto every soldier that pipes to it. And in the recesses of the porches, all day long, knots of men of the lowest classes, unemployed and listless, lie basking in the sun like lizards; and unregarded children, — every heavy glance of their young eyes full of desperation and stony depravity, and their throats hoarse with cursing, — gamble, and fight, and snarl, and sleep, hour after hour, clashing their bruised centesimi upon the marble ledges of the church porch. And the images of Christ and His angels look down upon it continually.

JOHN RUSKIN
The Stones of Venice, 1851–53

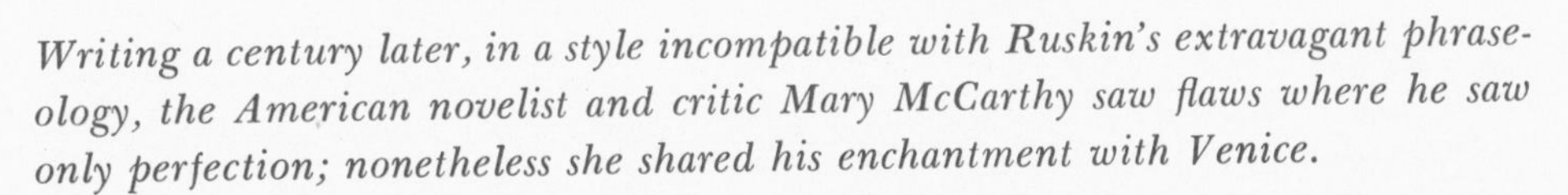

Writing a century later, in a style incompatible with Ruskin's extravagant phraseology, the American novelist and critic Mary McCarthy saw flaws where he saw only perfection; nonetheless she shared his enchantment with Venice.

St. Mark's as a whole, unless seen from a distance or at twilight, is not beautiful. The modern mosaics (seventeenth century) are generally admitted to be extremely ugly, and I myself do not care for most of the Gothic statuary of the pinnacles. The horses, the colored marble veneers, the Byzantine Madonna of the front, the old mosaic on the left, the marble columns of the portal, the gold encrustations of the top, the five grey domes with their strange ornaments, like children's jacks — these are the details that captivate. As for the rest, it is better not to look too closely, or the whole will begin to seem tawdry, a hodge-podge, as so many critics have said. The whole is not beautiful, and yet again it is. It depends on the light and the time of day or on whether you narrow your eyes, to make it look flat, a painted surface. And it can take you unawares, looking beautiful or horribly ugly, at a time you least expect. Venice, Henry James said, is as changeable as a nervous woman, and this is particularly true of St. Mark's façade.

But why should it be beautiful at all? Why should Venice, aside from its situation, be a place of enchantment? One appears to be confronted with a paradox. A commercial people who lived solely for gain — how could they create a city of fantasy, lovely as a dream or a fairy-tale? This is the central puzzle of Venice, the stumbling-block that one keeps coming up against if one tries to *think* about her history, to put the facts of her history together with the visual fact that is there before one's eyes. It cannot be that Venice is a happy accident or a trick of light. I have thought about this a long time, but now it occurs to me that, as with most puzzles, the clue to the answer lies in the way the question is framed. "Lovely as a dream or a fairy tale . . ." There is no contradiction, once you stop to think what images of beauty arise from fairy tales. They are images of money. Gold, caskets of gold, caskets of silver, the miller's daughter spinning gold all night long, thanks to Rumpelstiltskin, the cave of Ali Baba stored with stolen gold and silver, the underground garden in which Aladdin found jewels growing on trees, so that he could gather them in his hand, rubies and diamonds and emeralds, the Queen's lovely daughter whose hair is black as ebony and lips are red as rubies, treasure buried in the forest, treasure guarded by dogs with eyes as big as carbuncles, treasure guarded by a Beast – this is the spirit of the enchantment under which Venice lies, pearly and roseate, like the Sleeping Beauty, changeless throughout the centuries, arrested, while the concrete forest of the modern world grows up around her.

A wholly materialistic city is nothing but a dream incarnate. Venice is the world's unconscious: a miser's glittering hoard, guarded by a Beast whose eyes are made of white agate, and by a saint who is really a prince who has just slain a dragon.

. . . the Venetian mind, interested only in the immediate and the solid, leaves behind it, for our minds, clear, dawn-fresh images out of fairy tales.

MARY MCCARTHY
Venice Observed, 1956

Entrance to the Palazzo Surian

REFERENCE

Chronology of Venetian History

452	Attila the Hun levels city of Aquileia; refugees flee to islands of Venetian lagoon and found city
466	Lagoon community elects its first representative assembly
568	Refugees fleeing Lombards double lagoon's population
584	Enlarged assembly swears allegiance to the Byzantine emperor
697	Newly formed parliamentary council proclaims Venice a republic and elects first doge
810	Franks recognize Venetians as subjects of Byzantine Empire and concede trading rights on the Italian mainland
811	Seat of government moved to Rivo Alto, or Rialto, in mid-lagoon
814	First doge on Rialto, Agnello Partecipazio, orders construction of a ducal palace
829	Remains of St. Mark brought from Alexandria; Doge Guistiniano Partecipazio transfers patronage of city from St. Theodore to St. Mark; construction of the Doges' Chapel (later, St. Mark's Basilica) begun
976	Fire guts Doges' Chapel; St. Mark's relics mysteriously disappear
978	Construction of temporary basilica begun
997	Doge Pietro Orseolo II defeats Narentine pirates and conquers coasts of Dalmatia and Croatia
999	Holy Roman Emperor Otto III journeys to Venice and grants major commercial concessions
1063	Body of St. Mark rediscovered in basilica
1064–73	Basic permanent structure of St. Mark's Basilica completed
1095	Venetians lease their navy for First Crusade
1172	Responsibility for electing the doge transferred to the newly instituted Great Council
1177	Reconciliation between Holy Roman Emperor Frederick Barbarossa and Pope Alexander III mediated by Doge Sebastiano Ziani in St. Mark's Basilica
1202–04	Venice provides galleys for Fourth Crusade; Doge Enrico Dandolo leads navy; fall of Constantinople and establishment of the Latin Empire; Venice acquires Corfu, Crete, parts of Cyprus and Anatolia, and priceless Byzantine treasures
1253–99	Venice struggles with Genoa for Black Sea and Levantine trade; Venetians, victorious at Acre and Trapani, are ultimately defeated at Curzola
1275	St. Mark's Basilica completed; second Campanile, which was to stand until 1902, also finished
1297	The *serrata,* or "locking," of the Great Council; membership in the council restricted and made hereditary
1309	Enlarged Doges' Palace begun
1310	Bajamonte Tiepolo organizes an abortive revolt in protest against the *serrata*
1319	Libro d'Oro, or Golden Book, instituted; all births, marriages, and deaths of members of the aristocracy listed
1329	Campanile in Piazza San Marco refurbished
1335	Council of Ten, a committee of public safety, formed
1339	Venice captures Treviso and Castelfranco
1353–55	Second naval war with Genoa; Venetian fleet destroyed at Sapienza
1355	Newly elected Doge Marino Falier fails in attempt to gain public support against the aristocracy and is executed
1356	Council of Ten issues Sumptuary Laws regulating daily life and manners of Venetian citizens
1379–81	Third war with Genoa; blockade of Venice fails
1402–08	Venice conquers Padua and Vicenza, gaining control of the Lombard plain and access to the Alpine passes
1420–34	Ca' d'Oro, home of the Contarini family, built
1420–99	Further expansion on mainland; Friuli, Bergamo, Rovigo, Cremona annexed
1424	Façade of Doges' Palace overlooking the Piazzetta completed
1430–1516	Life of Giovanni Bellini
1441	Buon brothers decorate the Porta della Carta, main entrance to Doges' Palace
1452	Ca' Foscari, residence of Doge Francesco Foscari, built on the Grand Canal
1453	Venetians give Byzantine emperor minimal aid against Ottoman Turks; fall of Constantinople
1457	Doge Foscari deposed by the Council of Ten
1463–79	First war aganst the Turks; by terms of treaty, Venice pays annual tribute for right to trade in the Ottoman Empire

1477–1576	Life of Titian
1478–1510	Life of Giorgione
1480–1517	Procuratie Vecchie built in Piazza San Marco
1489	Acquisition of Cyprus
1496–99	Clock Tower built in Piazza San Marco
1508	European powers organize the League of Cambrai to prevent further expansion of Venetian Empire
1510	League of Cambrai temporarily occupies Venetia
1516	Venetian Jews restricted to the Ghetto
1518–94	Life of Tintoretto
1537–54	Sansovino Library completed
1537	Formation of the Council of Three; brief naval war with Turkey ends in a stalemate
1570	Turks besiege Nicosia, capital of Cyprus
1571	Turks are defeated at the battle of Lepanto by an alliance of Venice, Spain, Genoa, and the papacy
1573	Venice loses Cyprus to Turks
1574	King Henry III of France pays state visit
1574–77	Fires damage interior of Doges' Palace; reconstruction begun by Antonio da Ponte
1584	Procuratie Nuove completed in Piazza San Marco
1592	Rialto Bridge completed
1606	Venice briefly placed under papal interdiction
1617	So-called Spanish Plot to conquer Venice discovered and foiled
1629	Plague ravages Venice
1630–86	Construction of the ex-voto Church of Santa Maria della Salute
1643	First permanent opera house in the Western world opened in Venice
1645–69	War with Turkey over Crete
1669	Venice surrenders Crete to Turkish fleet
1685–87	Venice reconquers some Peloponesian ports
1718–96	Period of internal peace; tranquillity along boundaries of shrunken Venetian Empire
1780	Giorgio Pisani, procurator of St. Mark's, exiled for plan to overthrow aristocratic government
1797	Napoleon occupies Venice; Great Council meets for the last time; end of the Venetian Republic
1798	Venice ceded to Austria
1805	French regain control of Venice following the battle of Austerlitz
1810	Construction of Fabbrica Nuova, the Napoleonic wing of the Procuratie Vecchie, completed
1814	Congress of Vienna cedes Venice to Austria
1846	Rail causeway to mainland built
1848	Revolutionary leader Daniele Manin expels Austrians and establishes a republic
1849	Austrians reoccupy Venice
1861	Kingdom of Italy proclaimed with Victor Emmanuel of Sardinia as king
1866	End of Austrian domination of Venice; city joins the Kingdom of Italy and becomes capital of the Veneto region
1902	Campanile of St. Mark collapses
1912	Rebuilt Campanile inaugurated
1914	Italy proclaims its neutrality at outbreak of World War I
1915	Italy enters war against Germany and Austria-Hungary; despite later bombardment, no major damage to Venetian monuments
1917	Creation of new industrial zone and port of Marghera on western *barene* of the lagoon
1918	Italy ratifies the Treaty of Versailles
1922	Fascist "March on Rome"; Benito Mussolini forms cabinet and is granted dictatorial powers
1931	Automobile causeway linking Venice to mainland completed
1937	First all-Vivaldi concert in modern times held in Venice, the composer's native city
1940	Italy enters World War II by declaring war on France and Great Britain
1945	Benito Mussolini assassinated by Italian partisans; Allied troops liberate Venice, which had been spared major damage during war; German divisions in Italy surrender
1951	Population of Venice declines drastically; Giorgio Cini Foundation established
1960	Marco Polo Airport built at Venice
1966	Disastrous flood causes $64,000,000 in damage
1969	International University of Art founded
1971–72	International consortium of banks provides funds for massive renovation and restoration of Venice
1972	Special safeguard legislation for Venice introduced in Italian parliament

Guide to Venice

Arriving in Venice to undertake an assignment for *The New Yorker,* the noted American humorist Robert Benchley cabled his editor in mock horror: "Streets full of water. Please advise." As any visitor to Venice can attest, Benchley's wry observation deftly lampoons the city's most unique and extraordinary feature — a network of some 378 bridges and 150 canals that joins the 118 islands of the Venetian Rialto into a single city.

There is more to Venice than watery thoroughfares, however; scattered along the side canals and massed on both banks of the Grand Canal that bisects the city are scores of palaces, museums, and churches — famed for their exterior design, interior decoration, and historical associations.

The same aristocrats whose mercantile acumen enabled them to amass fortunes for their heirs left Venice itself a more enduring legacy — their opulent palazzi. Built in Byzantine, Gothic, Renaissance, and baroque styles — and in eclectic combinations of all four — many have been converted into public museums. Three such homes stand midway between the Piazzale Roma (at the head of the Grand Canal) and the Rialto Bridge.

The **Palazzo Vendramin-Calergi,** on the left bank, is an outstanding example of early Renaissance architecture. Built in the early sixteenth century, it later became the temporary residence of the German composer Richard Wagner, who died there in 1883. The massive **Palazzo Pesaro,** on the opposite bank, was begun by Baldassare Longhena in the 1660's and completed, with modifications, by Antonio Gaspare in 1710. The broad windows, fluted pillars, and carved stonework on the façade are an appealing framework for the treasures of the Gallery of Modern Art and the Oriental Art Museum within. Built for the Contarini family between 1420 and 1434, the **Ca' d'Oro** once glittered with gold leaf. Perhaps the finest Venetian Gothic palazzo, its asymmetrical façade is adorned with lacy openwork screens and ogival windows. Although the magnificent exterior decoration has faded, the structure itself has been fully restored and houses a fine collection of objets d'art, Roman busts, tapestries, and paintings.

Until 1854 the only bridge spanning the Grand Canal was the **Ponte di Rialto,** immortalized in William Shakespeare's *The Merchant of Venice.* Between 1588–91, Antonio da Ponte replaced the succession of precarious wooden bridges that had spanned the canal with the marble arch still in use today. Once the center of a bustling commercial empire, the stalls in the district's markets now sell mainly food produce. The bridge itself is lined with shops catering to tourists.

Farther down the canal on the left is the **Palazzo Grimani,** designed by Michele Sanmicheli in 1556. Its somber stone façade was once decorated with brilliant friezes. Also on the left are the **Case dei Mocenigo,** three separate houses unified by a single façade of white stone adorned with lion's-head reliefs.

Venice's devotion to commerce did not preclude piety; there are more than one hundred churches in the city. One of the most renowned is located north of the Case dei Mocenigo. Santa Maria Gloriosa dei Frari, known as **I Frari,** was begun in 1340 but not completed until more than a century later. The restrained reddish-brown brick façade is in keeping with the simplicity of the Franciscan friars who commissioned the church. The light and airy interior boasts two masterpieces of Venetian art: Giovanni Bellini's 1488 triptych and *The Assumption of the Virgin* by Titian on the high altar. Monuments to Titian and the sculptor Canova are also in I Frari.

At the western end of the church square is the **Scuola di San Rocco,** designed by Bartolomeo Buon and completed by Scarpagnino in 1549. Wealthy lay associations formed for charitable or religious purposes, the Renaissance *scuole* were responsible for erecting many distinguished structures in Venice. On the walls and ceilings of the white marble San Rocco is an incomparable series of fifty-six canvases by Tintoretto, including *The Annunciation, The Massacre of the Innocents, The Adoration of the Magi,* and *The Crucifixion.* One of several artists invited to submit designs for the interior, Tintoretto won the competition through a combination of ingenuity and talent: he awed his patrons by painting an actual ceiling panel instead of merely entering a sketch.

At the reverse bend of the Grand Canal stands the imposing four-story **Palazzo Foscari,** begun by Doge Francesco Foscari in 1452. For the royal visit of Henry III of France in 1574, the red brick palazzo was adorned with cloth of gold, silks, and velvets. Next to it, two mid-fifteenth-century Gothic structures comprise the **Palazzi Giustiniani.** In one, Richard Wagner composed part of his opera *Tristan und Isolde;* in the other, the American novelist William

Dean Howells wrote his *Venetian Life*. The nearby **Ca' Rezzonico** is perhaps the most opulent palazzo on the canal. Begun for the Buons in the 1660's by Longhena, it remained unfinished until the Rezzonico family acquired the property early in the eighteenth century. Pillars, columns, and sculptural reliefs adorn the façade. Today the Ca' Rezzonico houses a civic museum of eighteenth-century furniture and a collection of paintings, including a series of Tiepolo ceiling frescoes.

Although all of Venice could be considered a museum, there is an official gallery of art, the **Accademia,** in the former church and convent of Santa Maria della Carità on the right bank of the canal. Among the Venetian artists represented in the Accademia are Giovanni and Gentile Bellini, Giorgione, Carpaccio, Titian, Tintoretto, Tiepolo, Guardi, Bassano, and Veronese.

A single-arch wooden bridge erected in 1932 connects the Accademia to the left bank and the **Teatro la Fenice,** the oldest and largest theater in Venice. Destroyed by fire in 1836, it was subsequently reconstructed according to the original 1790 design. Such operas as Verdi's *Rigoletto* and *La Traviata* were first produced in the theater's pink and gilt auditorium.

Dominating the mouth of the Grand Canal is the **Church of Santa Maria della Salute.** Designed by Longhena in 1631 and constructed over the next fifty-seven years, this masterpiece of baroque ecclesiastical architecture commemorates the end of a plague that ravaged Venice in 1629. La Salute's huge, white marble dome makes it one of the most conspicu-

ous monuments on the island. Within the octagonal church are frescoes by Titian and Tintoretto.

Beyond La Salute is the **Dogana,** or customhouse — and directly south of it is the Giudecca, a series of eight islands linked by bridges. The chief monument on the Giudecca is the **Church of Il Redentore,** also erected to commemorate the end of a plague. Begun by Andrea Palladio, the church was consecrated in 1592. Stairs lead from the water directly up to the entrance; the façade is a neoclassical composition of pediments, pilasters, and other elements.

The **Church of San Giorgio Maggiore** is on the small island of San Giorgio Maggiore, east of the Giudecca. The red brick and white marble edifice, begun by Palladio in 1566, is the architect's greatest work in Venice. Four massive columns flank the entrance, and inset statuary adorns the intricate façade. A cultural institute, the Giorgio Cini Foundation, occupies the remainder of the island.

Directly across the lagoon from San Giorgio Maggiore is the **Church of San Zaccaria,** a Gothic structure with a six-tiered Renaissance façade capped by a semicircular pediment. Within is a beautiful altarpiece by Giovanni Bellini.

A leisurely stroll along the fashionable Riva degli Schiavoni, the esplanade that forms the northern perimeter of the basin of St. Mark's, leads to the **Piazzetta,** a small square fronting on the water that functions as the entranceway to the fabled Piazza San Marco.

At the threshold of the Piazzetta are two massive, red granite pillars. Atop one is a statue of the Greek St. Theodore, Venice's first protector; surmounting the other is a bronze winged lion, symbol of the city's patron, St. Mark.

On the west side of the Piazzetta is the **Sansovino Library,** designed by Jacopo Sansovino in 1536 and completed in 1588 after his death. Within the Renaissance building are rare antique books, and paintings by Veronese and Tintoretto. Opposite the library is the Doges' Palace, which extends into the Piazzetta proper.

The **Doges' Palace,** once the official residence of the chief magistrates and the seat of government, incorporates several earlier, smaller structures. In its present form it dates from the fourteenth and fifteenth centuries. The Piazzetta and quayside loggias — one austere and Gothic, the other delicate and Renaissance — were completed in 1424. These loggias, combined with a crenellated roof and a pink and white marble façade, give the palace a fairytale appearance.

The entrance to the courtyard of the palace is through the Venetian Gothic **Porta della Carta,** executed by the Buon brothers between 1438–42. Above the gateway are statues of Doge Foscari and the ubiquitous Lion of St. Mark. The courtyard's Renaissance façade was designed by Antonio Rizzo, who also planned the monumental Staircase of the Giants. At the head of the stairs are Sansovino's colossal statues of Mars and Neptune.

Within the palace the steep Scala d'Oro (Golden Staircase), adorned with gilded stucco reliefs, leads to the ducal apartments. Two serious fires in the 1570's destroyed the upper floors and their complement of paintings by Titian, Veronese, and Pisanello. The rebuilt High Renaissance interior, by Antonio da Ponte, contains masterpieces by Carpaccio and Bassano, a ceiling panel by Veronese, and Tintoretto's *Paradiso.* Suspended over the Rio di Palazzo is the infamous **Bridge of Sighs,** which connects the Doges' Palace to the prisons.

The marble pavement of the trapezoidal **Piazza San Marco** is bordered on the north by the **Clock Tower,** a charming fifteenth-century structure capped by two bronze figures that strike the hour of the day, and by the sixteenth-century, three-story **Procuratie Vecchie,** the former residence of the procurators of St. Mark. To the south is the **Procuràtie Nuove,** begun in 1582 by Palladio's pupil, Vincenzo Scamozzi, and completed by Longhena in the seventeenth century. Since 1830 it has housed a part of the Civico Museo Correr, Venice's civic museum. The two procuratie are joined on the west by the neoclassical Fabbrica Nuova, completed in 1810 during the French occupation.

The eastern end of the piazza is dominated by St. Mark's Basilica. At the southwest corner of the church is the graceful fourteenth-century **Campanile,** surmounted by a steeple and a gilded angel. The tower collapsed in 1902 and was replaced ten years later with an exact replica. At the foot of the Campanile is a small Renaissance loggia, designed by Sansovino in the sixteenth century. It was damaged when the tower collapsed but has been reassembled with the original materials. Four statues — of Apollo, Peace, Mercury, and Minerva — grace the structure.

The jewel of the piazza — and of all Venice — is **St. Mark's Basilica.** The original structure, built in the ninth century to house the sacred relics of St. Mark, was destroyed by fire. Although still referred to as a basilica, the present church — built between 1063–94 — was designed in the form of a Greek cross, capped by a 42-foot-high central dome with smaller domes over all four arms.

The architecture of St. Mark's is a tribute to Byzantium; but the exuberant embellishment of the façade is an inspired blend of Venetian, Romanesque, and Byzantine motifs. A profusion of disparate elements — Oriental spires, columns, canopied niches, statuary, and bas-reliefs — form a surprisingly harmonious whole. Five arched entrance portals beckon the worshiper and the tourist. Of the original mosaics that adorned the exterior, only the one over the north door dates from the thirteenth century; the rest, including *The Last Judgment* in the central lunette, are later additions. On the parapet are four massive bronze horses plundered from Constantinople during the Fourth Crusade.

No less impressive is the dim, cool interior of St. Mark's. Four thousand square yards of golden mosaics on the walls, vaults, and domes depict scenes from the Old and New Testaments. On the high altar is the priceless Pala d'Oro, or Golden Altarpiece, composed of gold and silver plaques and jeweled enamels. In the treasury is a rare collection of icons, ornaments, plate, and reliquaries.

The surpassing beauty of St. Mark's — a product of centuries of creativity — is perhaps the greatest legacy of the once-mighty lagoon republic.

COMMITTEES TO SAVE VENICE

FRANCE

Comité Français pour la Sauvegarde de Venise: Extensive restoration of the Church of Santa Maria della Salute.

GERMANY

Stifterverband für die Deutsche Wissenschaft: Major restoration of the Church of Santa Maria dei Miracoli; restoration of Tiepolo frescoes in I Gesuiti.

ITALY

Italia Nostra: Restoration of the Casette Lanza and the monument to Colleoni.

Comitato Italiano per Venezia: Major contributions to the restoration of the churches of San Stefano, San Donato (Murano), and Il Redentore; restoration of the Scuola di San Giorgio and the Convento dei Frari.

Societa Dante Alighieri: Restoration of the Arsenale.

UNITED KINGDOM

Italian Art and Archives Rescue Fund: Comprehensive restoration of the Church of La Madonna dell' Orto, including works by Tintoretto.

The Venice in Peril Fund: Restoration of the Sansovino loggia and the Church of San Nicolò dei Mendicoli.

UNITED STATES

Committee to Rescue Italian Art: Major contributions to the restoration of the churches of San Moisé, San Zaccaria, and Santi Giovanni e Paolo; contributions to restore frescoes by Veronese, Friso, and Liberi in various Venetian churches.

Venice Committee — International Fund for Monuments: Restoration of the façade of Ca' d'Oro; major contribution to the restoration of works by Tintoretto in the Scuola di San Rocco; restoration of Gentile Bellini's *Madonna and Child* in the Church of La Madonna dell' Orto.

Kress Foundation: Restoration of the Church of the Visitation and Tiepolo frescoes; contribution to pay salaries of technicians at Laboratòrio di San Gregorio.

Save Venice, Inc.: Restoration of churches of San Giovanni Crisotomo and I Gesuiti, and Levantina Synagogue; restoration of paintings in San Trovaso and mosaic floor of San Donato (Murano).

Selected Bibliography

Berenson, Bernard. *The Italian Painters of the Renaissance.* London: The Phaidon Press, 1967.
Burckhardt, Jakob. *The Civilization of the Renaissance in Italy.* London: The Phaidon Press, 1951.
Feist, Aubrey. *The Lion of St. Mark.* Indianapolis: The Bobbs-Merrill, Co., 1971.
Grundy, Milton. *Venice Recorded.* London: Angus & Robertson Ltd., 1971.
Morris, James. *Venice.* London: Faber and Faber Ltd., 1960.
Pignatti, Terisio. *Venice.* New York: Holt, Rinehart and Winston, 1971.
Rowdon, Maurice. *The Silver Age of Venice.* New York: Praeger Publishers, 1970.
Shaw-Kennedy, Ronald. *Art and Architecture in Venice.* London: Sedgwick & Jackson Ltd., 1972.
Steer, John. *A Concise History of Venetian Painting.* New York: Praeger Publishers, 1970.
Vasari, Giorgio. *Lives of the Most Eminent Architects, Painters and Sculptors of Italy.* New York: Simon and Schuster, 1946.

Acknowledgments and Picture Credits

The Editors make grateful acknowledgment for the use of excerpted material from the following works:

Death in Venice by Thomas Mann. Translated by Kenneth Burke. Copyright 1930 by Alfred A. Knopf, Inc. The excerpt appearing on pages 147–48 is reprinted by permission of Alfred A. Knopf, Inc.
Journeys in Italy by Théophile Gautier. Translated by Daniel Vermilye. Copyright 1902 by Brentano's. The excerpt appearing on page 144 is reproduced by permission of Coward, McCann & Geohegan, Inc.
My Life by Richard Wagner. Copyright 1911, 1939 by Dodd, Mead & Company. The excerpt appearing on page 141 is reproduced by permission of Dodd, Mead & Company.

The Editors would like to express their particular appreciation to Adam Woolfitt in London for his creative photography, and to Lydia H. Schmitt in Rome and Dr. Georgio Lauro in Venice for their invaluable assistance. In addition, the Editors would like to thank the following organizations and individuals:

Hiroshi Daifuku, UNESCO, Paris
The Hon. Mario Ferrari-Aggradi, Minister of State-Owned Industries, Rome
Prof. Roberto Frassetto, Laboratory for the Study of the Dynamics of Great Masses, Venice
Col. James A. Grey, International Fund for Monuments, Venice
Prof. John McAndrew, Save Venice, Inc., Venice
Barbara Nagelsmith, Paris
Prof. Renato Padoan, Superintendent of Monuments, Venice
Prof. Terisio Pignatti, Vice Director of the Museums of Venetian Art and History, Venice
Lynn Seiffer, New York
Dr. Vieri Traxler, Italian Consul General, New York
Prof. Francesco Valcanover, Superintendent of Fine Arts, Venice
Countess Anna Maria Cicogna Volpi, Venice

The title or description of each picture appears after the page number (boldface), followed by its location. Photographic credits appear in parentheses. The following abbreviations are used:

(B) — Osvaldo Bohm, Venice
(C) — Cameraphoto, Venice
(ME) — Marzari, Claudio Emmer, Venice
AW — Adam Woolfitt
MC — Museo Correr, Venice
U(DR) — UNESCO (Dominique Roger)

ENDPAPERS Mosaic floor in St. Mark's Basilica, 15th century. (ME) HALFTITLE Symbol designed by Jay J. Smith Studio FRONTISPIECE The city flag and the domes of St. Mark's. AW **9** Two of the four bronze horses on the parapet of St. Mark's Basilica. AW **10–11** The Rialto Bridge and the Grand Canal. AW **12–13** The Piazza San Marco, from *Pereginationes in Terram Sanctam,* by Bernardus de Breydenbach, 1486. Biblioteca Marciana (AW)

CHAPTER I **15** Relief of the Lion of St. Mark. MC **16** Marshy area on the island of Torcello. AW **17** Bronze gilt plaque of a Lombard horseman, *c.* 600. Bernisches Historisches Museum **18** Santa Maria Assunta and Santa Fosca, on the island of Torcello. AW **19** Mosaic of the Virgin and Child in Santa Maria Assunta, 12th century. (CE) **20** Miniature of Charles IV and Pope Innocent VI recalling the donation of Pepin to Pope Stephen II. Vatican, Libre Armaricum XXXV cod 20 fol 8 **21** Frankish helmet, *c.* 600. Reinisches Landesmuseum, Bonn **22–23** top, Gilded copper helmet decoration of King Agilulf, *c.* 590–615. Museo Nazionale, Florence (Mauro Pucciarelli); bottom, Silver-gilt hen and chicks, from the treasury of Queen Theudelinda. Cathedral Treasury, Monza (Mauro Pucciarelli); left, Jeweled cross, from the funerary crown of King Agilulf, *c.* 615. Cathedral Treasury, Monza (Mauro Pucciarelli) **24** Statue of St. Theodore, in the Piazzetta. AW **25** Statue of the Lion of St. Mark, in the Piazzetta, Persian, 4th century. AW **27** *Transportation of the Body of St. Mark,* panel from a polyptych, by Paolo Veneziano, 1345. Museo di San Marco (C)

CHAPTER II **29** Relief of a lion, from the island of Torcello. AW **30** Two of the four bronze horses on the parapet of St. Mark's Basilica. AW **31** Mosaic of St. Mark's Basilica, in the left portal of the same church, 14th century. AW **33** The domes of St. Mark's Basilica. AW **34–35** Two motifs from the bronze doors of the central portal of St. Mark's Basilica. Both (B) **36** top, Mosaic of Noah and the Dove, from St. Mark's Basilica, 13th century. AW; center, Mosaic of an angel, from St. Mark's Basilica, 13th century. AW **36** bottom, Mosaic of Noah and the Flood, from St. Mark's Basilica, 13th century. AW **36–37** left, Central detail from the Pala d'Oro, 10–14th centuries. St. Mark's Basilica (Editorial Photocolor Archives); right, The Nicopeian Madonna, 12th century, St. Mark's Basilica (ME) **38–39** Four reliefs of the Labors of the Months, from the central portal of St. Mark's Basilica, *c.* 1240. All AW **40** The Golden Staircase at the Doges' Palace, 1555–59. (ME) **41** La Bocca di Leone, from a corridor in the Doges' Palace. AW **42–43** St. Mark's Basilica, the Doges' Palace and San Giorgio Maggiore. AW **44** Relief of *The Drunkenness of Noah,* from the Doges' Palace, 15th century. AW **45** Capital showing the human race, from the Doges' Palace, 14th century. AW **46** The Rialto Bridge, 1588–91. AW **47** Detail of a miniature of Venice, from Marco Polo's *Les Livres du Graunt Caam, c.* 1400. Bodleian Library, Oxford, Ms. 264 fol 218.

CHAPTER III **49** Lion from the Clock Tower in the Piazza San Marco, 1500. AW **50** Relief of St. Mark, from the door of a Bucentaur. (B) **51** left, Two fragments from a Bucentaur. (B); right, Gilt and wood model of a Bucentaur. Museo Storica Navale. (B) **52–53** left, Panel of St. Sebastian, from a polyptych by Giovanni Bellini in Santi Giovanni e Paolo. (ME); center, *Procession of the True Cross in St. Mark's Square,* by Gentile Bellini, 1496. Accademia (Garanger/ Giraudon); right, *Doge Giovanni Mocenigo,* by Gentile Bellini, 1478–85. MC (ME) **54** *Doge Loredan,* by Giovanni Bellini. Accademia (B) **55** left, *Portrait of a Young Man,* by Giovanni Bellini. Metropolitan Museum of Art, Jules S. Bache, 1949; right, *Saint Dominic,* by Giovanni Bellini. National Gallery, London **56** *Madonna of the Oranges,* by Cima da Conegliano. Accademia (Nimatallah) **58–59** top, *St. Ursula's Dream,* by Vittore Carpaccio. Accademia (ME); bottom, Detail of the meeting of the virgins and St. Ursula with Pope Cyriacus, by Vittore Carpaccio. Accademia (Editorial Photocolor Archives); right, *The Vision of St. Augustine,* by Vittore Carpaccio. Scuola di San Giorgio degli Schiavoni (C) **60** Bust of Doge Foscari, by Antonio Bregno, *c.* 1440. Doges' Palace Museum (B) **61** Ca' Foscari. AW **62** *The Tempest,* by Giorgione. Accademia (C) **64** Relief of a galley, from a bench on the island of Torcello. AW **65** Bronze statue of Bartolomeo Colleoni, by Andrea del Verrocchio, 1481–88. Campo dei Santi Giovanni e Paolo. AW **66** *Healing of the Demoniac,* by Vittore Carpaccio. Accademia (Giraudon) **67** Cantino chart of demarcation, 1592. Biblioteca Estense, Modena (Mauro Pucciarelli)

CHAPTER IV **69** Lion from the Scuola Grande di San Marco, c. 1495. AW **70–71** left, Interior of the Biblioteca Marciana, by Jacopo Sansovino, 1540–80. AW; right, Exterior of the Biblioteca Marciana. AW **72–73** Detail of a woodcut of the procession of the doge in the Piazza San Marco, by Mattia Pagan, 1556–69. MC (B) **74** *Due Dame Veneziane,* by Vittore Carpaccio. MC (ME) **75** *Man in a Red Hat,* attributed to either Lorenzo Lotto or Vittore Carpaccio. MC (ME) **76** Engraving of Henry III entering Venice, 1574. MC **78** *Doge Andrea Gritti,* by Titian. National Gallery of Art, Washington, Samuel Kress Collection **79** *The Assumption of the Virgin,* by Titian. Church of I Frari (ME) **80** Engraving of the Hall of the Great Council in the Doges' Palace, by G. B. Brustolon after a painting by Canaletto, 18th century. MC **81** *Portrait of a Venetian Senator,* by Tintoretto. National Gallery of Art, Washington, Chester Dale Collection. **82** left and right, Two frescoes by Paolo Veronese at the Villa Barbaro, Maser. (B) **83** Villa Barbaro, Maser, by Andrea Palladio, 16th century. (B) **84–85** *Feast in the House of Levi,* by Paolo Veronese. Accademia (Nimatallah) **87** San Giorgio Maggiore. AW **88** *Battle of Lepanto,* by Paolo Veronese. Accademia (C) **89** Relief of a sea battle, from the Church of San Clemente. (B) **91** Map of Venice, by Ignazio Danti, *c.* 1550. Galleria delle Carte Geografiche, Vaticano (Mauro Pucciarelli)

CHAPTER V **93** Lion from a gondola pole outside Ca' Rezzonico. AW **94** The Bridge of Sighs. AW **95** Pennant from the galley of F. Morosini. MC (B) **96** Plan of Santa Maria della Salute, by Ferrazzoni. MC **97** Santa Maria della Salute. AW **98–99** Main altar in Santa Maria della Salute. (B) **101** Chandelier in Ca' Rezzonico. (ME) **102** Perspective of Ca' Rezzonico. MC **103**

Drawing of an ambassador's boat, 1689. Biblioteca Marciana (B) **104** *The Embarkation,* by Giovanni Battista Tiepolo. Palazzo Labia (C) **105** Sketch for *The Embarkation.* (Giacomelli) **106–07** Four cherubs from the main altar of Santa Maria della Salute. (B) **108–09** *Piazza San Marco,* by Canaletto. Musee Jacquemart-Andre, Paris (Josse)

CHAPTER VI **111** Lion doorknocker on a Venetian house. AW **112–13** top, *Il Ridotto,* by Gian Antonio Guardi. Ca' Rezzonico (ME); bottom, *Il Parlatorio,* by Gian Antonio Guardi. Ca' Rezzonico (ME) **114–15** Four paintings of 18th-century Venetian life, by Pietro Longhi, at Ca' Rezzonico. From left, *The Morning Chocolate, The Doughnut Girl, Family Concert, The Rhinoceros.* All (B) **116** *The Coronation of Doge Alvise IV . . . at the Doges' Palace,* by Francesco Guardi. Louvre **117** *Festivities in the Piazzetta on the Last Thursday of Carnival,* by Francesco Guardi. Louvre **118** left, *Pulcinella and Clowns,* by Tiepolo. Ca' Rezzonico (B); right, *Pulcinella's Swing,* by Tiepolo. Ca' Rezzonico (B) **119** *Pulcinella in Love,* by Tiepolo. Ca' Rezzonico (Giacomelli) **120–21** *The Minuet,* by Tiepolo. Louvre **122** Engraving of Napoleon's arrival in Venice, 1807. MC **123** Engraving of the removal of the bronze horses from St. Mark's by the French. MC **124–25** left, The collapse of the Campanile, 1902. (Giacomelli); right, The Campanile reduced to rubble, 1902. (B)

CHAPTER VII **127** Lion from the door handle of a water taxi. AW **128** left, High water in Piazza San Marco, 1968. Unesco; right, Freighter moving past San Giorgio Maggiore. U(DR) **129** Collapsed bastion at the Fort of Sant' Andrea on Vignole Island at the Lido entrance. U(DR) **130** Marble statue from the Doges' Palace. (C) **131** Marble statue supporting drainspout on St. Mark's Basilica. (C) **132** Restoration workshop at Pontecasale. U(DR) **133** left, Restoration of Paolo Veneziano's *Virgin and Child.* U (DR); right, Professor Pedrocco restoring a painting by Piazzetta in the Church of Santi Giovanni e Paolo. U (DR) **135** Gondola prow and the Grand Canal. AW

VENICE IN LITERATURE **136** Cover of the commissioning of Doge Alvise Mocenigo, 1703. MC (B) **138–60** Twelve sketches of scenes and events in Venice, by Francesco Guardi, 18th century. **138** Piazzetta of San Marco. MC **140–41** Piazza San Marco. Petit Palais, Paris **142** Masked Venetians. MC(B) **144–45** Opening of the Teatro la Fenice, 1792. MC(B) **146–47** The basin of St. Mark's. MC **148–49** Burning of San Marcuola, 1789. MC **150–51** The frozen lagoon. MC **152** Festival boat. MC **154–55** Piazzetta of San Marco. Louvre **156–57** The Rialto Bridge. Musee Epinal **158–59** Bucentaur and fleet sail towards Sant' Andrea. MC **160** Visit to the Palazzo Surian. MC

Index